STUMBLING
IN THE LIGHT

STUMBLING IN THE LIGHT

New Testament Images
for a Changing Church

Robert Kysar

Chalice Press®

St. Louis, Missouri

Biblical quotations, unless otherwise noted, are from the *New Revised Standard Version Bible*, copyright 1989, Division of Christian Education of the National Council of Churches of Christ in the USA. Used by permission.

Cover artwork and design: Mike Foley
Interior design: Rhonda Dohack
Art direction: Michael Domínguez

This book is printed on acid-free, recycled paper.

Visit Chalice Press on the World Wide Web at
www.chalicepress.com

10 9 8 7 6 5 4 3 2 1   99 00 01 02 03

Library of Congress Cataloging–in–Publication Data

Kysar, Robert.
　　Stumbling in the light : New Testament images for a changing church /
by Robert Kysar.
　　　　p.　　cm.
　　ISBN 0-8272-3441-4
　　1. Church—Biblical teaching.　2. Change—Religious aspects–Christianity.
3. Bible. N.T.—Criticism, interpretation, etc.　I. Title.
　　BS2545.C5K97　　1999　　　　　　　　　　　　　　　99–38563
　　262—dc21　　　　　　　　　　　　　　　　　　　　　　C1P

Printed in the United States of America

*Dedicated
with gratitude to
all the agents of change
in the church today*

Contents

Acknowledgments

Finding the headwaters of a river is often very difficult. Identifying the beginnings of a stream of thought is just as difficult. One can name major influences—those larger streams that feed a tiny trickle and eventually sweep it along, but you remain embarrassed that you cannot always acknowledge seminal beginnings. Sometimes, as familiar ideas present themselves, the lines of dependence become so blurred the thoughts seem to be your own.

Still, I must acknowledge a number of those who have influenced my thought and enabled the research for this book. I have avoided the temptation to document every possible source for the materials in these chapters. To do so would encumber the reader with innumerable pages of notes. Instead, I have used the notes only to direct you to other publications you might want to examine. To the many who remain unmentioned in the notes but who have aided my thought, I express my indebtedness and gratitude.

My colleagues at Candler School of Theology and the Graduate Division of Religion of Emory University are also among those who have shaped this book. Working among and with such stimulating partners has stretched my mind and enriched my life. I am grateful to Candler for granting me a sabbatical leave for the academic year 1996–97 and for making possible a period of that leave at Cambridge University. Moreover, Candler generously provided me with the services of a research assistant during the previous academic year. The Reverend Ms. Nickie Stipe aided me enormously with a bibliographical search, and she also raised probing questions that helped me think and speak more clearly about this project. In many ways, she has modeled the postmodern Christian woman for me and thereby allowed me a vision of the future of the church. Professor Jonathan Strom kindly converted the electronic version of the first draft into a contemporary word processing program that made revisions much easier. Ms. Sandra Tucker kindly prepared most of the index for me.

I am also deeply indebted to all the "agents of change" who live and work within the church. Their courage and perseverance have emboldened me to undertake the writing of this book. I tremble to think what the church in North America would be today without their continuous efforts to keep the community of faith engaged with its culture. This book is dedicated to them with my thanks!

Not least of all, it has helped tremendously to live with a pastor who serves a congregation struggling with change. My wife, the Reverend Dr. Myrna Kysar, encouraged my efforts to address the issue of change and the church. Lest I forget my own years as a pastor, her immediate experience with congregational change and resistance to it anchored me in the real life of the congregation—the heart of the church. To all these persons I express gratitude and appreciation.

Introduction

It all seemed so obvious. The tiny congregation gathered in a building many times larger than its needs. It had once been a prosperous middle-class neighborhood church in a small metropolitan area. But, like so many congregations in comparable situations, it dwindled away as the neighborhood around the building changed. Members moved out to the suburbs, and most transferred their membership to congregations near their new homes. A few, however, clung to the beloved old church. Each Sunday they drove from their comfortable suburban homes to their church in what had become an ethnically mixed and economically lower-class neighborhood.

As their new pastor, it all seemed so obvious to me. The congregation must begin to reach out to the residents of its neighborhood. Doesn't every congregation want to do that? Isn't every congregation mandated to do that? Indeed, in this case, the congregation's very existence depended on its doing so.

So I tried to foster programs targeted at those who lived around the church building. With the help of a seminarian, we visited the homes of people near the church and developed a mid-week after-school program for the children of the neighborhood (mostly Hispanic), some of whom lived as close as across the street from the church. We wanted the church building to become a friendly place for residents of the neighborhood. As obvious as it all seemed, however, the congregation's members saw no purpose in these new outreach programs. "Those people" never came to worship on Sunday mornings. They made no financial contributions to the church. Those who supported the church were the elderly, middle-class, white suburbanites who came from afar to worship there. With determination the laypeople clung to the past and often expressed their

1

fond memories of what used to be. A classic story of the urban church in the late twentieth century!

My efforts to effect change in that congregation were, I believe, nearly total failures. The members did not want change. They desired most of all the survival of the status quo, as grim as that was. I wondered then and even now why they were so resistant to change, especially when conditions made the necessity of change so obvious. As their pastor, what might I have done to foster a different attitude toward change?

The classic and common story of the older urban congregation is in some ways not unlike another congregation's story. In this case, the setting is suburban and the membership middle- to upper-middle class, again exclusively white and of European descent. They had a relatively short history, growing from a small gathering in a local schoolhouse to a substantial membership in a modern building. The congregation enjoyed a fruitful ministry with good pastoral leadership and attracted an abundance of gifted and bright professional people who were genuine in their commitment to Christ and his church. A pastor could hardly ask for more potential in one congregation!

Suburban growth continued to occur all around them, and this congregation enjoyed its share of new members over several decades. Their pastor's resignation, however, posed new problems and brought them to a critical time for vision and new orientation. They had outgrown their own self-understanding as a cozy "family church." The sheer number of members required new and diversified programming to serve a broader scope of interests and needs. A new pastor could not be expected to be the familiar face at every congregational event; programs could no longer expect to evoke the participation of every member. A judicatory representative invited the congregation to begin to think of themselves as a different kind of church, one in which laity were more and more responsible for events and in which not everyone knew everyone else as a member of the "family." Would they become a new church for a new age in their community?

Like the urban congregation's response to my efforts to lead it into ministry to its new neighborhood, some in this suburban congregation resisted the change. They wanted to remain the congregation they had been when only a hundred members dreamed of a church building of their own. They had come to think of the church as an institution that served their needs and were now reluctant to think of themselves as servants of others. They sought to maintain the self-understanding nurtured in their beginnings without recognition of the changes they had experienced. Again, it was all so obvious! A congregation of their size could no longer be a closely knit family of like-minded people. Yet even the obvious was not sufficient reason for change.

As different as they are, both congregations exemplify a resistance to change, and both cause us to ask why. Why does the church in general, and congregations in particular, find change so very difficult? When change is inevitable, when it is clearly demanded by the church's setting, when it is God's call to new ministry, why even then is it so painfully hard? Is the church destined to cleave to the past no matter what the present, much less the future, might be?

Those questions comprise one of the two personal reasons for this book and the starting gate for my reflection. On the one hand, as one committed to the church's ministry, I had long wrestled with *the issue of corporate change in the faith community*. The stories sketched above are representative of my years as a pastor in a number of congregations. Every one of those years heightened my sensitivity to the way in which change threatens our lives. I observed and participated in numerous efforts to effect change both in congregations and in the broader expressions of the church, only to watch those efforts fail. Within the last decade it became clear to me (as it has to many) that our culture is in the midst of a radical transition—what some have even called the beginnings of a "postmodern" age. These cultural changes may very well challenge even the church's existence in our society. As a community, how might we deal with this mutation in faithful and healthy ways? What might be done to equip the church for change?

On the other hand, in the last several years I have become increasingly interested in *metaphor*. Actually that interest roots in an earlier fascination with the metaphorical nature of theological language. That same fascination was aroused again by the emergence of the new literary methods of biblical interpretation. Those experiences connected with my study of the ways in which metaphorical language functions in preaching and thereby focused my attention on the role of metaphor both in the biblical text and more generally in Western consciousness.

The convergence of these two interests and commitments gradually formed the beginnings of a thesis that provides the basis of this volume. We live by metaphors in the sense that they provide semi-conscious interpretative lenses for experience. Basic, foundational metaphors define our identity as individuals, but also as communities and especially as a community of faith. Such metaphors are most often culturally determined, inherited through conditioning, and seldom surface for critical examination. Often we would not be able to articulate the metaphorical language that gives life and breath to the church. However, with the new understanding of the role of story in human self-understanding, we have edged closer to recognition of the basic images that shape both individual and corporate identity.

The importance of metaphor and the church's resistance to change furnished two building blocks in the foundation of this book. But there are still three more such blocks that became the footings of its structure. As I reflected on resistance to change and the role of metaphor in forming communal identity, I realized that *the most common images for the church's nature and function had little to do with change.* Often the metaphors by which we conceive the church are those that do not sufficiently emphasize the roles of process and discovery. They are instead images of stability, strength against the forces of the world, or an anchor in the storms of change. To be sure, in some congregations we hear the community described as a "pilgrim people." I fear, however, that expression has been personalized and used almost exclusively for individual spiritual search rather than for the community of faith. The need for images of change is the third building block.

For the most part, it seems the church has been unsuccessful in nurturing a corporate identity that deals effectively and in healthy ways with change. So, how might that process be improved? Here is where a fourth building block is needed for this project. The New Testament is saturated with metaphors for the church. The first century was a crucial period during which the Christian community struggled to discern its identity within various cultural settings. In that context the community's leaders fashioned verbal pictures of the church, many of which are accessible to us through the writings of the New Testament. Moreover, the earliest church was in a constant state of change. It began as a movement within Judaism; then it became a predominately Gentile community. The community first nurtured relationships with the Roman empire (e.g., Rom. 13:1–7). In time, however, Christians experienced the evil face of Roman power. Rome became, at least for some Christian communities, the incarnation of Satan (e.g., Revelation).

Therefore, along with faith, logic leads us to a reconsideration of the images of the church found in its earliest writings. Among them we are most likely to find at least the stimulation to create new metaphors that visualize the church as a dynamic organism. Those New Testament images themselves may not work as successfully as they originally did. They may need to be translated into contemporary language. They may be only the sparks that ignite the fires of our imaginations, but in any case the New Testament's language for the church supplies us with some construction materials.

Our *challenge* is to mine the New Testament for resources out of which we can begin to fashion new images for the church—ones that empower the church for change. This is the fifth building block of this book. The task is to incorporate into our communal consciousness metaphors for the church as a community on a journey with change. To accomplish that task we balance ourselves between two worlds, standing with one foot planted solidly in the soil of our culture and with the other on New Testament earth. Our project will falter if we lose footing in either. The new images for communal Christian identity can neither simply parrot the Bible nor imitate our culture. They must instead translate biblical images into the language and modes of thought of twenty-first century North American culture. Moreover, those new images need to be ones that have potential for empowering us for change. In the midst of the cultural transformation in North America, the church needs metaphors that allow the community to interpret experiences of change in productive ways—in ways that find promise rather than only threat in change.

This book therefore assumes at least five basic assertions: The church today resists change. Communal identity is formulated in metaphors. Most current images of the church fail to help us deal constructively with change. The New Testament language for the church is our basic resource for image building. Our challenge is to fashion new dynamic images for our day and time out of biblical ones.

I do not claim that a reclamation of New Testament metaphors for communal change is a quick fix for all that ails the church. We will not easily accomplish the process of appropriating and integrating such new self-understanding; the issues entailed in the church's transition into the new century are far more complicated than my thesis. But this book aspires to ignite a new interest in the examination of the metaphors by which the church lives. If these pages contribute in any way to that process, I shall be more than satisfied.

The goals of this project are to present selected New Testament images of the church as a dynamic and changing community, to convince the reader that these images were formative of early Christian identity, and to assess the promise of such imagery for contemporary Christian communal self-understanding in a time of change.

The argument of the following chapters is relatively simple. In brief, it moves from our current envelopment in change to the role of metaphor in identity, then to some New Testament images for the church, and finally to the cultivation of new images in a congregation. The chapters will proceed through these four stages. Chapter 1 will explore the reality and threat of radical cultural change for the immediate future of the church. Here we will examine briefly the current relevance of change for the church and the complexity of our resistance to change. Chapter 2 will introduce metaphor and its essential role in self-understanding. We will try to illumine the foundational role of metaphor in determining how humans view the world and experience. I will offer brief assessments of the adequacies of several current metaphors for the church that I hear used in congregations today.

Chapters 3, 4, and 5 are devoted to metaphors for the church in the New Testament. In the first of these three we will examine a portion of the Gospel of Luke and the Acts of the Apostles in order to study the metaphor "on the way." In the journey theme of Luke-Acts we will look for the discoveries the disciples and the first church found along the way with Christ and the Spirit. Chapter 4 turns to a number of passages that speak of the Christian community in the process of seeking its divinely destined home. Chapter 5 examines other New Testament language that implies Christian knowledge is not static but dynamic, growing, and changing. The examination will, first, take us inside Jesus' announcement of the "kingdom of God" and, second, lead us into the metaphorical world of Paul's theological language.

In the process of chapters 3, 4, and 5, I will mold these three images into one: On the way home, stumbling in the light. When that molding is complete, the full image may hold promise to shape a particular community self-understanding that expects and welcomes change where it is consistent with the gospel message. Together these three pictures of the church focus on possibilities for the future and might encourage us to anticipate and greet new visions of possible truth.

What will we do with all this in a congregational setting? Chapter 6 responds with some concrete strategies for planting and nurturing new images in the lives of parishioners. We will ask whether the New Testament metaphors provide raw materials for constructing viable and useful metaphors for individual congregations. In particular, will they empower us to deal more constructively with change? Then the chapter will suggest how to facilitate new images through preaching, Bible study, and congregational administration. One goal of this final chapter is to invite you to think about how the use of new metaphors for the church's identity sparks still others in the minds of your parishioners.

Along the way, I invite you to test the assumptions and thesis of this project against your experience in the church and to evaluate my readings of biblical texts by means of your own interpretations. I hope that the basic images of Christian communal life operative in your life and ministries will surface. Writing this book has had that salutary effect on me, and I hope readers will share my experience. I hope too that you—informed by the biblical images—will be stimulated to conceive and nurture your own new and contemporary metaphors for a changing church.

CHAPTER ONE

A Season of Change

My father-in-law, Martin, died in 1992 at the age of ninety-nine. Soon after his death my wife and I reminisced about Martin's life. We thought about all the changes he had experienced in the course of his near century of life. At first we began listing the innovations of the period but soon despaired, for they were so numerous. Martin lived his whole life in the context of an unbelievable swirl of change.

Koheleth, the teacher, muses, "For everything there is a season and a time for every matter under heaven" (Eccl. 3:1). Today the sage might well speak of "a season of change." Looking back over the twentieth century, few would deny that we are in such a season. Many of us find it hard to imagine that technological breakthroughs of only two or three decades ago are now replaced with still newer developments. Of course, like every season of change, this one has proven itself ambiguous. For all the optimism of the early part of the twentieth century, we have learned that so-called progress is dangerous. In a single century we have unleashed the power of the atom, probed the universe beyond our planet, and devised the microchip. But we have also witnessed two world wars, the atomic bomb, and the most thorough and deliberate genocide known in human history. Seasons of change are as frightening as they might be exciting.

The church has a history of difficulty in dealing with change. A perusal of the church's history makes clear that we have tended to resist change, both within the ecclesiastical institution itself and in the cultures of which the church has been part. Even the New Testament witnesses to such resistance. The expansion of the church's mission to the

Gentiles was not easily achieved, as Luke suggests in the Acts of Apostles and Paul makes even more explicit (Acts 15 and Galatians 2—see chapter 3). That difficulty in dealing with change extends through the centuries down to our own. Within the past several decades alone, we have experienced the church's struggle to come to grips with abortion, homosexuality, and women's ordination, to name just a few examples. The church does not deal well with change.

What then of the future? How will the church fare in a new season of change? How can we manage change in ways that are faithful to our calling as a people of God? The investigation of these questions begins in this chapter with a three-part discussion. The signs of the radical change close upon us in the twenty-first century provide a point of beginning. That analysis then requires a brief examination of the challenge the church faces in such a season of change and most especially some reasons for the church's reluctance to welcome cultural and communal change. Finally, this chapter introduces a proposal for equipping the church for a drastic season of change.

Signs of a Season of Change

Any analysis of cultural change, both present and future, is fraught with difficulty. There is no purely objective observer of culture, nor is there an omniscient mind that knows the future with certainty, especially a future born out of change. This discussion attempts little more than to summarize my observations, tainted by my own agenda and prejudice and accompanied by only my best hunches about the future of North American culture. Let readers use this discussion to evoke their own analysis and anticipation.

The End of a Season of Contentment

The concluding third of the twentieth century signaled even more radical change than we had experienced in earlier decades. Ironically, the church had no sooner begun to find its legitimate and faithful place in a modern and secularized culture than the cultural critics began speaking of a new cultural era, now commonly called postmodernism. The church struggled severely with the emergence of modernity out of the Enlightenment period. Out of that struggle came what many called an accommodation and what others claimed was a new mission. Christian apologetics found ways to respond to modernity with at least some degree of theological integrity. Developments in scientific inquiry have even been claimed as resources for Christian life and faith. The church not only adjusted to a therapeutic culture[1] but availed itself of the riches of such an environment. Science and religion seem to have matured beyond their initial alienation to the stage of mutual discourse we witness today.

So shaped by and comfortable with modernity did we become that some christened the twentieth century the "Christian century."[2] The church purchased stock in the enterprise of progressivism, believing that, along with human knowledge and welfare, Christian faith would thrive and increase in the decades to come. The emergence of theological liberalism with a peculiar North American flavor signaled a profound Christian compliance to what had begun as a threatening chaos of change. The church welcomed modern culture as an ally, not a despised opponent.

But the happy wedding of the two became troubled by the middle of the twentieth century. The two world wars and the Holocaust played decisive roles in disrupting the relationship. While its impact was slow in reaching the United States, Karl Barth's seminal commentary on Romans bespoke the dissolution of the happy marriage of the church and modern Western culture as it had been blessed in Europe. Neo-Orthodox theology reclaimed the church's stance over against culture, but in doing so betrayed its failure to address modernity in full measure. The Holocaust produced a still more lasting dissolution of the harmony between church and culture. An evil of such proportions could not be dismissed; business as usual could not continue, at least never in the form of liberalism. Theology after Auschwitz became, and remains, a haunting refrain that will not be quieted.

In North America during the 1960s and 1970s theological reflection seemed for a time to dissolve into fragments, torn apart by multiplicity and disparate directions for the future. Existential thought bred individualism in a day of increasing acknowledgment of the social quality of life. Demythologization, first offered as a method of addressing the modern age, conceived its illegitimate offspring in the short-lived "death of God" movement. In the dense fog of the United States' involvement in Vietnam, social and political rebellion in North America surfaced fundamental questions that were never resolved, such as the issue of authority. The advent of the racial movement for freedom brought us unwillingly before a cultural mirror, and we did not like what we saw there. The limited success of that movement in the succeeding decades challenged all that we once thought was honorable about Americans. The feminist movement added fuel to the same fire. Women could never return to their pre–World War II status as subservient creatures, but neither could we visualize—much less realize—a new relationship of equality between the genders.

Since partially recovering from our decade of greed in the 1980s, we have been in search of a new national identity as a people. A global economy broke the back of national privatism; ethnic identity disclosed the lie of the melting-pot image; and the end of the cold war deprived us of our convenient scapegoat—something to which our national personality had become addicted through the period of the "cold war." All this was only aggravated by what we had first greeted with unbridled enthusiasm—the revolution in communication. Television at first seemed the best thing ordinary North Americans had seen since the automobile; but gradually we began to recognize its wasteland. The monster created out of our own genius rose up to threaten us. The telephone seemed marvelously to close geographical distances, only to be followed by the microchip and computer. Communication has become so easy that now we sometimes yearn to be excommunicated! These ingenious creations threaten to numb us to one another.

Amid this historical context, suddenly we found ourselves on the brink of something very different from the modernity to which we had become so accustomed. The best we could say was that we seem to be on the verge of a "post-something-or-other." We must speak of the future as an unknown about which we can say only that it will be different from the past. Postmodern, postliterate, postliberal, and even post-Christian have all been used to speak of that frontier on which we stand. The church made its peace—even if it was an uneasy peace—with modernity; now it must face the churning waters of disruption once again. If some critics are correct, our season of content is about to be transformed in the foul weather of postmodernity.

Perplexing Pluralism

Within the swirl of anticipated change, one thing seems most certain about the new century before us. It will be an era of human diversity and multiplicity, the likes of which North American culture has never known. All pretenses of cultural homogeneity have been irreversibly revealed for what they always were, namely, suppressions of differences into a Western European mold. Theology has sometimes named the era to come as the age of the "other,"[3] meaning that those who are different from the majority, or simply from ourselves, will figure prominently in our lives.

The North American church has participated in the suppression of diversity in subtle but effective ways. We have conveniently divided ourselves into congregations of "like-minded persons" and into wider divisions (called denominations) in terms of socioeconomic classes.[4] Racial, ethnic, class, and other differences were "managed" through disguised segregation. Witness, for instance, the way in which different denominations tried to respond to the emergence of racial identity and pride. In some cases, special institutional structures were created to accommodate African American "brothers and sisters." In other cases, we have been content to allow them to have "their church" and we ours. In the closing decades of the twentieth century, guilt sent the major denominations scrambling to "include" persons of different races, ethnicity, and languages within their midst.

Racial, ethnic, and language diversity is, however, only one form of the pluralism awaiting us. To some degree the Christian church is learning to live with diversity within itself, but we have often been less interested in dealing with those of entirely different religious traditions. Yet the signs of a season of change are evident. Closely associated with the acknowledgment of racial and ethnic diversity is the revival of traditional ethnic religions. The reclaiming of traditional African religious practices and beliefs among African Americans may be an indication of what is to come in the future. Racial, ethnic, and language traditions cannot help but revitalize religious systems in which they are historically rooted. Native Americans have reappropriated their rich religious and spiritual traditions, sometimes in relation with Christianity and sometimes independently. We would only be guessing if we tried to predict what new ethnic religious expressions might emerge in the future, but surely they will challenge the church to find its authentic relationship with such religious forms.

So, too, will the church be asked to reposition itself with regard to the classical religions of the world.[5] The presence of Buddhists, Muslims, and Hindus steadily increases in the midst of what the older generations always assumed to be a "Christian nation." A Buddhist lives two houses down the block; a Hindu appears as a guest in the front pews at a Christmas Eve service; the pastor's spouse is an African American Muslim. The globalization of population, coupled with the attractiveness of the spirituality of other religious systems, assure us that the church's culture in the twenty-first century will be religiously diverse.

Furthermore, the proliferation of novel religious forms, already witnessed in the varieties of "New Age" views, is likely to continue and even increase. There is little reason to think that such religious and quasi-religious phenomena will diminish, even if some of them are only reflections of the cultural anxiety excited by a period of transition. Modernity spawned the freedom to cultivate and even invent new forms of religious practice. In the atmosphere of postmodernity, we can be assured that the freewheeling human spirit will continue that tradition. In some ways, these new religions may be products of the quest for a deeper dimension in a radically secularized society;[6] in other ways they reflect a deep dissatisfaction with traditional Christianity, at least in its institutional forms. Postmodernism promises to question the basis of modernity's secularization and may very well open avenues for new ways of knowing truth, the result of which will accelerate the growth of the new religious forms.

Finally, the pluralism of the new age will entail the emergence of a new agnosticism and relativism. The Enlightenment freed our ancestors from the oppression of the established church, and atheism and agnosticism became live options suppressed in former periods of Western culture. For reasons that will be discussed below, the postmodern age promises at least initially to make forms of agnosticism and relativism attractive. The disguise of certitude, cultivated first by the church and then by early science, may be stripped away, and certainty made less and less attainable. In such an atmosphere those whom we have often labeled the "unchurched" will multiply. Life's meaning will have to be carved out of contentment with knowing less and less about reality as a whole. Larger, universal systems of belief may be unnecessary to render human existence purposeful. Perhaps we will witness something like a kind of agnostic nihilism (i.e., unknowing nothingness) functioning in the place of religion. Possibly newer forms of humanism (without the trappings of the idealization of the human spirit it had in modernism) will also emerge. In whatever form they present themselves, we may assume that the church will find itself living in and confronted by a society in which religious convictions seem to many to be unnecessary and finally impossible ways of life.

Powerful reactionary movements have resisted the new pluralism of North American culture at the close of the twentieth century. The controversy over prayer in public schools, for instance, seemed once to have been resolved, only to resurface again in the politics of the 1990s. The reactionary character of the renewed controversy suggests that the dominant culture of North Americans does not want to acknowledge the reality of diversity within its society. Mixed in with the resistance to recognize the pluralism of religious orientation entailed in school prayer are a good many other prominent political issues at the close of the century, each of which entails an effort (however it might be disguised) to deny diversity—to restore the traditional family as it was once known in this nation; to suppress the homosexual population; to restrict immigration to a nation that was fashioned by a variety of immigrants and that once prided itself in harboring those from other nations; to abolish legal efforts to correct past injustices against racial minorities and women; and to restore a set of values embraced by the dominant culture of the early 1900s. We seem to be in a state of cultural denial, refusing to acknowledge the very existence of the "other" in our midst, even when the others may be destined to outnumber the once dominant culture. Denial is but one way of trying to resist inevitable change.

Perhaps the reality of pluralism in the United States is the most significant of the several reasons for what some are calling the end of "Christendom." For over two hundred years, the Christian church in the United States has enjoyed a privileged relationship with the state. In spite of the constitutional separation of church and state, a general and vague kind of Christianity has tended to function as the norm for North

American culture, with values allegedly rooted in the so-called Judeo-Christian tradition. Consequently, as our culture has been forced to acknowledge its diversity, some traditional moral values have begun to disintegrate and the privileged role of Christianity to dissolve. The efforts of groups like the "Christian Coalition" in the last decade are evidence that Christendom in the United States has been fatally undermined by religious pluralism. The ramifications of such a shift in relationships between the church and culture are variously assessed, but it seems likely that the church will be forced into a new role. That role, I believe, is properly understood as something closer to what the church experienced in its origins before the emperor Constantine.[7]

How will the church deal with pluralism in the twenty-first century? The so-called *other* has already become a theme in theological reflection among those who take the signs of a season of change seriously.[8] Pluralism asks the church to examine its view of and relationship to those who are in some way different from ourselves. The church has usually cultivated an imperialistic tolerance of others who believe differently. Imperialism views them as candidates for conversion. Christians are responsible for leading them to the truth, assuming, of course, that the church has a unique claim to the truth denied others. Tolerance, too, assumes that the other is misled, inferior, and incapable of knowing all that we know. To tolerate others is to admit that we would rather they not exist at all but that we will allow them to suffer the consequences of their ignorance.

Can the church find a way to change its posture toward the other, to recognize the otherness that already resides among us, and even to acknowledge the otherness within us as individuals? The pluralism that promises to be the church's cultural environment for the next century tempts us to construct a new sectarianism, a withdrawal from culture for the sake of self-preservation. Such a sectarianism, however, mitigates against the church's mission in the world and infects us with a deadly disease that slays Christian love and care. What resources are there to cultivate a willingness to risk genuine dialogue with those whose views and lifestyles differ from our own?

Media Mentality

The potent pluralism of our culture in the twenty-first century involves a change in the church's cultural setting. Media mentality involves a change within us. It denotes a fundamental transformation of human consciousness, perception, and cognition. This transformation has been helpfully compared with the one inaugurated by the invention of the printing press.[9] That pivotal development brought to a conclusion centuries in which people perceived and learned primarily through hearing and speaking and initiated an age in which we would learn through the printed word. The postmodern age has been called post-literate in the sense that reading the printed word will no longer be the primary way of learning and that a new kind of visual orality would carry the day—an orality that combines both hearing and seeing. The change that concerns us in this section is a fundamental mutation in the kind of people we are, regardless of how we might judge that change.

There are a number of media influences on us that reshape the manner in which we learn and process information and consequently alter our self-consciousness. The two most powerful of those influences are television and the computer.

Television. Once television production had grown beyond visual radio, it began gradually to discover the power of visual images. Today a single evening of television viewing treats us to a myriad of visual experiences. Programs are designed to move quickly, and necessarily superficially, through their subjects. In a matter of seconds news programs leap from the scene of an incident to a dozen or fewer words spoken by an interviewee and back to the reporter. Interviews on the network morning programs are conducted within brief and tightly controlled time allotments, often leaving the viewer with only the most general impression of a topic. The plot lines of dramas and situation comedies unfold swiftly from problem to resolution. Subplots intensify and diversify the action, even though they may be only loosely related, if at all, to the theme of the central story. The impression is that viewers are incapable of concentrating on a single plot line and must be moved quickly back and forth among the major and subplots.

The infamous commercial "breaks" are perhaps the most revealing aspects of the television medium. In a few seconds the commercial must grab viewers' attention and then inject them with the advertiser's message. Learning must take place in a matter of seconds. In their quest for viewer attention, producers of television commercials resort to ingenious ways of moving from the "grabber" (e.g., the beautiful woman and handsome man engaged in some tantalizing activity) to the message (e.g., we would be much better off if we wore a certain brand of denim trousers) and, in the worst cases, make no pretense of creating a logical relationship between the two. Sometimes the commercial does little more than create a warm atmosphere of contentment and then associate the product with such an atmosphere.

Among other things, television has produced two vital changes in our mentality.[10] First, it tends to fragment our learning into tiny bits. Producers are obsessed with the viewers' attention span, but, in their concern to do everything in short bits, they have in fact shortened the normal attention span and magnified their own challenge. Many television experiences leave viewers on their own to form some order out of the unrelated fragments to which they have been subjected. For instance, how are we to find a unifying theme among the plot and subplot lines of a one-hour drama? The result of this is that our way of learning, of processing the knowledge we gain from viewing experiences, is being transformed. We seem left with one of two options: Either to remain content with the sheer pleasure of the tiny and unrelated experiences or to construct our own framework by which we integrate them into a whole. The latter is likely to become less and less probable the more common and frequent television viewing becomes and the more the medium itself becomes the message. Hence, the emerging mentality is one content with mere fragments of knowledge without larger structures. Larger structures of meaning become less and less necessary to the enjoyment of experiencing tiny momentary pieces of information or entertainment.[11]

A second lasting influence of television on us is that it creates a thirst for immediate satisfaction. Plots must move quickly to please us and must be filled with action, for viewers have been conditioned to expect a rapid pace. It is, then, more than our attention spans that have been altered by television; it is our aesthetic sense of what is pleasurable. We grow impatient with that portion of a plot that sets up characterization, restless with lengthy analysis of political and social conditions, and annoyed by dialogue without action.

Computer. In some ways, the computer promised to be very different from television. With it we could write the lengthy essay or analyze data in a magnificently varied number of categories. The printed page was, at first it seemed, simply transferred to the monitor screen. But at least three developments appear to have allied the computer with television. One of those three is the simple speed with which this marvelous machine does its work. Once again, our willingness to attend to lengthy tasks has been diminished as the operating speed of computers and programs incessantly increases.

Far more complicated, but also far more important, is the Internet. In a matter of minutes it can deliver vast amounts of information in the convenience of our homes. We could learn more than we ever wanted to know about any given subject, thanks to the material available on Web sites and to the manner in which one collection of information invites seeking related discussions found only a few mouse moves away. Unfortunately, that promise has often gone unfulfilled, perhaps due less to the fault of the sources than to the patience and interest of many users. The Internet is perhaps most often used in the same fashion as one reads the news in a copy of *USA Today*. The substance is found in the first few lines, making it unnecessary for all except the vitally interested to go further. Networking sources of information has turned into "browsing"— superficially scanning rather than broadly comprehending. Or, sensational topics receive the most attention, much like television news plays to our thirst for sensationalism. A cultural analyst might argue that television had already spoiled us before the Internet got hold of us.[12]

Still a third development in computer capabilities has transformed its promise. With the rise of the Internet has come the integration of the computer with both television and telephone. Computer devices attached to our television now enable us to access the Internet in our living and family rooms. Making the new information highway so easily accessible is promising but also entails some dangers. Accustomed as we are to television viewing, will the computer now become an extension of the fragmentation initiated by television?

Results. In addition to television and the computer, this new mentality has doubtless taken form under the influence of other media. Newspapers, for instance, following the lead of *USA Today*, have gone to shorter articles with accompanying graphics. The fast pace of plots found in current motion pictures seeks to satisfy the impatience of television viewers. The musical video flashes a variety of images, however incongruent they may seem with the lyrics and musical theme. The cause and the consequence of the new mentality are mixed. The greater our need for fast information becomes, the more the media increases it.

Both television and the computer have tended to compromise our willingness to experience long and analytical treatments of issues and exacerbated the fragmentation of knowledge. These media train us to process information in microbits, to devalue extended or deeper understandings, and to become comfortable with the fragmentation of truth itself. Consequently, they have transformed our senses. The broader result is that we may become more content with life as small, discrete pieces of experience without regard to the relationships among them.

One analysis of the illiteracy of the present age and the subsequent decades defines illiteracy as the inability to read extended documents. It is not that we cannot read; it is that we will read and comprehend only short statements. If that analysis is sound, the postmodern age may be one in which mentality is attuned only to foci without concern for context or questions of causes and consequences. Might such a mentality produce human consciousness with little or no grounding in the past and minimal concern for the future? Will such a consciousness weaken the capacity to transcend the present moment to ask questions of causes and consequences? Most frightening, will such a consciousness find images of the whole of reality, both religious and philosophical, a waste of time?

Of course, the media as a whole has accustomed us to instantaneous information in great abundance. The combination of news television networks with the computer Internet has made possible the global communication of events within minutes after their occurrence. We are privileged to be in touch with our world in new and immediate ways, the likes of which astound any of us over fifty years of age. In addition to the availability of information and the knowledge it provides, the inter-active character of the computer (and increasingly of television) has jarred passive television viewers. We not only have access to information but are participants in resourcing the information, as well as to determining the course of a plot in a computer game or television program. Soon the North American mentality may not tolerate communication over which it has little or no control.

The Church and Media Mentality. The church is already trying to change its forms of ministry to accommodate this media mentality. Congrega-tions have introduced abbreviated twenty-minute worship services in order to attract those who want to be "churched" each week without the ordeal of a full sixty-minute service. Sermons are shortened; educational programs come packaged in brief segments with a variety of experi-ences and instantaneous relevance; complex topics are treated in digest forms. In future decades those kinds of changes will seem more and more necessary.

But what are the deeper implications of the media mentality for re-ligious faith and life? Christian faith purports to provide a unifying view of the whole of life, but will those afflicted with the fragmentation of knowledge be interested in such unity? We offer the Christian gospel as a sort of grand narrative that holds our various stories together, but can the media-saturated mind comprehend such a universal story? We have come to understand that human consciousness is formed around and through story, but will personal story survive the splintering of life and knowledge? Christian morality is concerned with both causes and con-sequences, but will the media mentality care about either? The need for instantaneous satisfaction surely has implications for a religious faith focused on God's yet unfulfilled promises.

Without losing its soul can the church change to conform to the new human consciousness emerging as a result of the media? What is at stake in such indulgence? The issue is not just can the church change but when and how it should change. Does the church's self-understanding lead it always to accommodate to culture, to stand over against culture, or to become a subculture in itself?

Eroding Assumptions

The questions evoked by the media mentality lead to and overlap with other kinds of sweeping cultural change potentially found in the new century. The questioning of assumptions that birthed and sustained modernism further condition the new human consciousness shaped by the media. What has come to be called postmodernism appears to threaten two broad and basic assumptions operative in modernity.[13]

How We Know. The first eroding assumption is that concrete evidence is the only sure path to knowledge (empirical epistemology). In its origin science offered marvelous opportunity for learning about our natural environment. So productive was the scientific method of learning that expectations of it became exaggerated until all truth was thought to be of the kind science studied. On the popular level, scientific data was the conclusive proof of truth and the basis for detecting falsehood. The scientific method constructed a castle within which the modern person could dwell in security.

But the castle has begun to crumble as weaknesses in its structure became evident, first to the scientists themselves and then more slowly to the general populace. Werner Heisenberg undermined the certitude of some sciences by challenging the quantum theory. Equally important, the objectivity of the scientific method was shown to be illusory. Theoretically scientific research was based on pure detached observation, but we have reluctantly learned that humans are seldom, if ever, capable of such objectivity. Various types of experiments could be used to "prove" numerous different propositions, depending on the design of the experiment and the financial profit it might yield. After buying toothpaste on the basis of scientific research, the modern layperson began to recognize that medical studies are sometimes inconsistent and inconclusive in their results. With increasing suspicion of the most current studies, many have begun to wonder about the validity of scientific research.

This is not to say that the world has not profited enormously from science nor that it will not continue to do so. Surely the newest ventures into genetics and even cloning will prove revolutionary. But the issue is whether the sciences are the simple answer to the quest for truth. In some circles postmodernism delights in debunking this basic assumption of modernity. Ironically, the church struggled for centuries to accept the historical-critical methods of biblical study, only to arrive at that acceptance and then have biblical scholars admit that there is no such thing as the objective, scientific, and unprejudiced reading of a biblical text. The demise of pretense that the observer could be objective accompanies the admission that the sciences can, at best, know only a small portion of whatever truth there is to be known.

While the church may be eager to applaud the fall of the sciences from their station high in the human temple, we should recognize that some less welcomed consequences also follow. If there is no objectivity possible in the quest for truth, that includes religious truth as well.[14] If scientific evidence in general is ambiguous, so is the evidence of religious experience. If science cannot discern truth from falsehood, is such discernment possible at all for us humans?

What We Can Know. The new view of the scientific method and its role in the quest for truth is but one of several features of the postmodern age that questions basic assumptions. The decades to come are liable to produce a greater and greater suspicion of theories that purport to be universal in their compass. With a new global sensitivity we can recognize that the universal truths that modern theories often propose are not total at all but strictly "Western." When we embraced views of human nature, for instance, the humans we had in mind did not necessarily include those who live south of the equator. With a sober recognition of the role of the theoreticians' personal biases and their social conditioning, postmodernism seeks to deflate grand theories that pretend to include all reality. Anticipating the prominence of such wariness of inclusive theories, Christian theologians are revisiting many of the classical doctrines of the church.[15]

Much the same can be said for the postmodern aversion to "metanarratives"—those stories that claim to encompass the individual stories of societies and individuals. Such stories simply "plaster over cracks in the projects of modernity."[16] One such metanarrative on which many others have been structured is the Hegelian story of the spirit that moves through all history, shaping and determining all that happens. Other grand narratives include the most basic religious stories. The popular view of the history of the "mighty acts of God," for instance, seems just such a metanarrative; it purports to be God's story for the salvation of all humanity. In practice, however, it may often systematically exclude some from the scope of divine salvation. How then are postmodern Christians to think about their faith, if not in terms of some grandiose divine plan for all humans? How does our understanding of our own faith experience function without declaring it to be normative in some degree for all persons?

Finally, postmodernism's challenge to both how we know and what we can know forces us to be honest about our vested interests as we discern what is true and what is false. The social and political power gained from positing certain things to be true has often proven more decisive than some innate desire to know truth. Humans are products of their social and political situations, and those situations seem to determine what we perceive to be true and what false. Hence, postmodernist thought may reduce our ability to know to what we *want* to know, not what truly is. Political implications saturate all human endeavors, so that finally we appear doomed to our vested interests and their advancement. Such a view seems cynical but may prove to be more realistic than we want it to be.

Of course, all this talk of a postmodern age may prove to be so much rubbish. Only time will demonstrate what, if any, truth there is in such analyses. Nonetheless, the church needs to be alert to the trends of which the postmodernists speak. What do they mean for Christian thought and practice? At worst it may mean that Christianity is propagated more for the political and social well-being of its adherents than for its inherent truth; at least it may mean that we Christians need to acknowledge the influence of our social and political condition on our religious perspective. We may, for instance, have to admit that advocating a particular moral view may be motivated as much to maintaining a comfortable status quo as it is to advancing values from which others may benefit.

I and We

Our thorough embeddedness in a social condition leads to another foundational assumption challenged by postmodernism that needs to be singled out here for special attention. That assumption roots in the distinction between the self and others and was supremely the result of Rene Descartes's philosophy. Some would argue that this distinction resides at the heart of modernity and that it will crumble under the powers of postmodernism. What is at stake in this distinction for the church and Christianity in general is the role of the individual in relation to the corporate body of society, as well as the very nature of human relations themselves.[17]

Postmodernism seems, on the one hand, to lead us toward a total relativism in which each individual discerns truth for her or himself and lives accordingly. On the other hand, some contemporary cultural analysts see evidence of a turn away from radical North American individualism toward a new communalism. Modernism tended to conceive society as the sum total of the individuals who comprise a social grouping. Postmodernism reverses that understanding and claims that individualism is for the most part the product of socialization. The individual is little more than a mirror reflection of the society in the context of which the individual lives. The slogan fostered by Descartes's "I think, therefore I am" might be rephrased "*We are*, therefore I am."

As we know it today in Christian thought, individualism probably originated in the period of the Enlightenment and especially in the wake of the pietistic movement. The individualism of pietism has influenced modern Christian thought in a manner equal to Descartes's influence on philosophy. North America has claimed such a view of the self as the cornerstone of its identity and spawned a Christianity in which the individual soul is a discrete and foundational reality. Consequently, community has proven more and more problematic in North American Christianity.

Postmodernism challenges us to acknowledge our bondage to others of our society in general and our separate subsocieties in particular, while forcing us to see ourselves primarily as corporate rather than individual entities. It leads us to think more in terms of group, to cherish relatedness with others, and to nurture our relatedness, but postmodernism may also challenge the absolute distinction between the "I" and the "thou," with the result that we will understand "I and we" from a new perspective. The other and I are to some degree one, regardless of what differences I may want to impose on the other. Commonality, then, becomes more essential to relationship than difference, similarity more definitive than uniqueness, interdependence more authentic than independence, and togetherness more real than separateness.

If such a view of human existence wins the day in the future century, the church must rethink much of its theology and its practice. The radical emphasis on my private relationship with God may be a facade behind which I can hide my own will to power over others. The uniqueness of my personality may be recognized less as a divine gift and more as a barrier to relationships with others in the community. One thing appears most certain about the postmodern Christian theology in the future: The gathering of the community of faith will become the essence of Christian practice and not simply a source for individual empowerment.

With these reflections on how postmodern thought may change our relationships with one another, the discussion has come full circle back to the pluralism with which it began. The "other" viewed in this light is hardly other at all, since you and I are glued together in an inseparable way. The "other" may not be another person whom we tolerate or disdain as much as that part of us that resists the unity we share with all other creatures. We ourselves are in effect "the other."

The Church in a Season of Change

The process of trying to name some of the radical changes that may await us in the next century has already raised some vital questions for the church and its place in a new age. But attention must now focus, not so much on the culture of which we are part, but on the church in such a cultural transition.[18] The church is generally resistant to change and has often been a conservative force in periods of cultural shifts. There are clear reasons for such reluctance to share in the changes of culture, some laudable and some unfortunate. A sketch of this reluctance entails investigating, however briefly, two related problems for a church that finds itself in the midst of a season of change.

The Church's Dilemma

First, the church's theological tradition, for the most part, puts it at risk in such a cultural transition as we face in our nation. Our theological stance is premised on a belief that we have been privileged to find God revealed in the person of Jesus of Nazareth. By the grace of God we have benefited from the divine Word enfleshed in human form and have been brought into a new relationship with our Creator. We then dare to say that through revelation the church gathers around a body of truth that is fundamental to human existence, a glimpse into the Ultimate Reality.

Over the centuries the church has guarded and passed on the treasure of that revelation through stories of God's saving activity and through creeds that articulated the essential content of the treasure. Through all the cultural transitions of two thousand years, the church has maintained that there is something unchangeable and precious in the faith "once delivered." To varying degrees care has been taken to distinguish between the faith itself and how it is to be lived and even understood in the particular cultural contexts in which the church found itself. But the apostolic faith is the bedrock on which the church stands, however cultural variations may necessitate new articulations of that faith. The church has withstood cultural change by clinging to that which is unchanging and eternal according to our faith. Consequently, in a period of cultural change the church must balance itself precariously on a narrow ledge. On the one side of that slender ledge is total refusal to recognize the culture and its changes; on the other side looms the precipice of an accommodation with culture that threatens complete identification of the church with its culture at the expense of the Christian tradition.[19]

The church cannot stand apart from culture, since it is inescapably a part of its culture. To speak its faith—even to understand it—Christianity has to do so within the context of a language, certain modes of thought, and symbolism—that is, within a cultural context. There is no Christian faith, no gospel, and no religious language that transcends culture. The church becomes pretentious the moment it claims to be acultural. As Christ's disciples we remain "in the world" (John 17:11). Moreover, the community of faith has a mission to its culture. So, however it may resist change, it must learn to speak the language, understand the values, and share the life of its culture. The church's whole ministry tries to interpret Christianity to its time, and in doing so is forced to speak a contemporary language. At the very least, in a season of cultural change the church is required to understand emerging values and share the discourse of the day, whether that means embracing the culture or standing over against it. The church's theology itself dictates the place of the community of faith in culture. The doctrine of the incarnation affirms that God's decisive revelation for humanity occurred in a single human within a specific cultural context. "The Word became flesh and lived among us" (John 1:14). God's Word inhabited history at a definite time and place. Because God's self-expression was within a cultural context, the church and its message is ever bound to its culture and time.

On the other hand, when the church admits its cultural nature, we are tempted to become nothing more than another expression of our society. To accommodate the faith entirely to the culture is to lose Christianity's distinctive contribution to humanity and sever our connection with the historic apostolic faith. Christ—the incarnate Word of God—challenged his culture, attacked its presuppositions, and revolutionized the world. Although he was part of his society, he never allowed himself to become nothing more than a product of that society. The doctrine of incarnation requires the church to be in a culture. But the ministry of the incarnate one models the church's relationship with its culture.

So, like a "fiddler on the roof," we try to keep our balance on this tiny pinnacle. Every cultural change necessitates learning some new balancing skills, since drastic cultural change always threatens our equilibrium. In every cultural transition in the history of the Western church one can find examples of portions of the church tumbling off the roof's peak in one or the other direction. How then shall the church maintain its balance in a postmodern era or something like it? For good reason the church is hesitant to follow its culture, and change must be made carefully. To quote our imaginary contemporary Koheleth again, "There is a time to change, and a time to remain the same."

Reasons for Resistance

Having viewed the dilemma produced by cultural change and the church's theological tradition, along with good reason for Christians to be cautious about change, the analysis moves to some other sources of reluctance to change within the church. These are far more personal and emotional than theological, but perhaps actually more powerful.

Of course, change of any sort tends to threaten humans insofar as it disrupts the security we find in continuity. In recent years psychology has studied stress among twentieth-century North Americans. One of the more fascinating findings of these studies is that it is not simply negative or unpleasant transitions that increase levels of stress. Change of any sort does so. Marriage, the birth of a child, promotion to a new job, or moving to a beautiful new house are all stressful in ways not unlike a divorce, the death of a loved one, or unemployment. Simply put, change is stress-producing because it scrambles the ordinary and disturbs the status quo.

Consequently, when change is initiated within the church, it emotionally dislocates people not unlike a geographical move might do. It places us in a new environment. To some degree, any variation of the "normal" forces us to reorient ourselves and asks us to abandon something we value. A vivid example of this occurred when, as a result of the Second Vatican Council, the Roman Catholic Church in the United States abandoned the Latin mass in favor of English. The shock wave that went through North American Roman Catholics at that time suggests how a single (and logical) change disturbed the practice of thousands of faithful Christians. Much the same thing occurred when denominations began ordaining women. All the popular models for the clergy were scrapped and new ones had to be fashioned. Worshipers found themselves in a strange and unknown place when a woman occupied the pulpit.

Moreover, the new often implies that the old is in some sense wrong. On the societal level, for many Christians provisions for the equal rights of gay, lesbians, and bisexuals imply a negative judgment on past attitudes toward homosexuals. In my pastoral work I discovered to my surprise that a congregation viewed innovation to be a condemnation of the past. For some the introduction of a new hymnal, for instance, suggested the inferiority of the old hymnal on which they had been raised. Change within the church seems to demean the value of the tradition, even when the innovation attempts to retain or even reclaim tradition.

This sketchy analysis of the threat of change helps us understand the common denial of transition and process among North American Christians. With remarkable refusal to acknowledge cultural transformation, many cling desperately to the past and what remains of it in the present without willingness to face social realities. Denial of reality is a way of coping with any experience that threatens emotional stability. However, we are likely to respond to change in a healthy way only when we acknowledge and deal directly with the realities of life. Denial of change often only prolongs its pain, and in the church's case delays its ministry to a new culture.

The total impact of change is negative in many cases because of the way in which it threatens us and implicitly questions the value of the past. James W. Fowler has studied the dynamics of change in personal maturation in terms of its impact on faith development. He speaks of four aspects of the "texture of transitions" in personal maturity, each of which is helpful in an analysis of the church in a season of change. Fowler views such transitions as "endings" of significant things for the individual. Those endings deprive life of the "sense" it previously had. First, transitions result in

> "*disengagement*," that is, an experience in which we are forced to give up a significant connection to some context of relationship and shared meanings that has helped to constitute our sense of self...*Disidentification* results from breaking or losing old connections with the world, which means the loss of important ways of self-identification...*Disenchantment* means giving up or enduring the loss of some part of our previous constructions of

reality...*Disorientation*, in a sense, is the cumulative impact of the other three aspects of our experience of endings...[Then] we find ourselves in...the *neutral zone*...When our time in the neutral zone has done its work, we begin to find the clues or the signposts that point toward the shaping of *new beginnings*.[20]

Fowler's discussion of personal transitions in maturation helps us understand corporate transitions, both in our culture and especially in the community of faith. The church has achieved a kind of comfort zone in North American modernity, which now is being disturbed by the transitions we are experiencing as a culture. There is about the present a sense of an ending, a conclusion to the existence the church fashioned for itself out of the violent storms of the onslaught of modernity. The present is filled with threats of the four textures of transition Fowler names.

Certainly the church is already experiencing the texture of disengagement. The relationship it has shared with its culture is being fractured. Change is shredding the meaning and values the church had in common with modern North American culture. The result is an emerging sense of confusion about Christian corporate identity. That disidentification means simply that, as a community within our culture, we are less sure of who we are and how we are to act. Corporate disenchantment for the church entails that our theological assumptions are challenged in new ways and that we may no longer be able to depend on them as adequate in a new century. Theology is our corporate construction of reality, and its very foundation is being scrutinized in new and disturbing ways. All this results in a kind of disorientation, a period of quest for new relationships and new images of reality, a period of new beginnings in a neutral zone. Can the church emerge from a process like this into a new comfort zone, or will the future require that the textures of transitions themselves become the only comfort zone we will ever again know?

Preparing for a Season of Change

If this a "neutral zone" in which we live (or may soon live), how do we begin to find clues and signposts for a new beginning? When a change of seasons approaches, we prepare ourselves. With the first signs of the advent of winter, we ready ourselves: Check the furnace and the antifreeze in the car, and find the snow shovel. Change of seasons requires preparation. The advent of a season of change, too, prompts preparation.

With the likelihood that the church is facing radical and prolonged change, the church needs to address some fundamental questions. Writing about personal Christian commitment, Margaret A. Farley claims,

> If we are not to be "unhitched" from our commitments, the se-
> cret is to hold together our past and our future, but to do so in a
> way that does not leave us with something static and unchang-
> ing. Only if we are open to new meanings for the past can we
> risk flexibility in our expectations of the future. Without this
> kind of flexibility, we cannot sustain hope.[21]

The issues confronting us are as basic as whether the church can sustain its commitment through a period of cultural transition.

First on our agenda of preparation is a new inquiry into the issue of change itself in our life together as Christians. If it is our self-identity that is at stake in the change facing us, we want to ask about the nature of Christian corporate self-identity. Much as transitions in individual lives surface the question of personal identity with brutal force, so too the radical season of change forces us to examine our corporate identity.

The question of how the church understands itself is complicated by two factors. On the one hand, all that has been said above indicates that our conception of who we are as the body of Christ in a drastically altered North American culture requires examination. If we find our-selves in a pluralistic culture in which the media mentality prevails, the church marginalized and its fundamental convictions challenged in new ways, how are we to imagine and express our mission and purpose? That question alone is overwhelming, but when it merges with the ques-tion of how we are to view change itself, our task is even more difficult. Is change always threatening and destructive of what Christians hold dear? Is change to be resisted at all costs? What should the role of change in our corporate self-understanding be?

This book does not pretend to answer all the questions raised by the discussion of the cultural transition in which we find ourselves. To pre-tend to do so would be simply arrogant. Instead this study narrows the issue to what seems to be the most pressing item on the church's agenda in a postmodern age, namely, our corporate self-understanding particu-larly as it relates to dealing with change. The next chapter argues that self-understanding is most often constructed out of mental pictures or images of ourselves. Specifically it explores the possibility that meta-phorical language is the fabric out of which identity is created. The dis-cussion then examines some images that currently function to help us comprehend our identity and evaluates their adequacy for the season of change upon us. After considering that possibility, we will be ready to ask how the earliest Christian communities forged their images for self-understanding in the monumental changes they experienced.

CHAPTER TWO

The Method of Metaphor

Change challenges self-understanding for communities as well as for individuals. In the context of the significant cultural change around us, the church has already begun to wrestle with its identity, asking, "Who are we?" But how is the task of discerning and articulating corporate self-understanding to be managed? What is involved in such an enterprise? Can corporate self-understanding *be managed*? Can we intentionally change the way we think of ourselves as a church? If that is possible, how do we accomplish it?

One way of responding to these queries is "the method of metaphor." Such a response requires consideration of several issues. At the heart of this chapter is the two-part question of how we conceive and articulate an understanding of corporate identity. With a proposed response to that question in mind, the chapter goes on to investigate several current understandings of the church in terms of their capacity to engage change. The final section provides a bridge to the investigations of a number of New Testament images for the church's self-understanding.

Self-identity and Metaphor

Individuals often express their immediate sense of identity in word-pictures. A friend of mine use to respond to my greeting "How are you?" by saying, "I feel like a million!" More likely is the use of such imaginative expressions when we are feeling depressed. Counselors often hear the confusion and despondency of others in utterances that include the word "like." "I feel like sh__!" "I feel like I'm in a dark hole and can't get out!" "I feel like I'm trapped!" Faced with having to summarize our individual self-understanding at any moment, we resort to metaphors—little word pictures that depend on comparison with something else. A million dollars, human excrement, a dark hole, or caught in a trap like an animal are all ways of pointing to a self-perception.

Maya Angelou provides a more poetic example of this feature of self-perception:

> *When I think about myself,*
> *I almost laugh myself to death,*
> *A dance that's walked,*
> *A song that's spoke, ...*[1]

The poet captures a dimension of her self-identity in metaphors: a joke, a dance, and a song. To conceive of ourselves and articulate that conception we employ the poetic qualities of language, especially metaphor.

Such a use of metaphorical language suggests several important things for this study. The first is that language is important. We conceive through words and their combinations. Language is more than merely a vehicle to express thought that is independent of words. It is, as one philosopher put it, "the house of being" for us.[2] Our lives themselves, as well as our thinking, are immersed in language.

The second insight we gain from considering our metaphorical self-expressions is that language itself seems limited but is in fact almost without limits. Individuals in a euphoric or a despondent mood cannot easily find words adequate to capture their sense of self-identity. But metaphor—comparing our sense of self with something else—taps an inherent richness in language. That is, metaphorical language pushes ordinary language beyond itself. What is most important about this practice is that our descriptive language fails us when it comes to such important issues as self-identity, and we resort to the poetic potential inherent in words. We cannot name ourselves the same way we name one structure "chair" and another "garage"; self-identity is too elusive for ordinary and purely descriptive language (if there is such a thing as purely descriptive language). But we can comprehend a sense of identity at any one moment in another kind of language that breaks free of description through new and odd associations of words and phrases: "My life has been one great big joke."

But, third, the practice of using metaphor to articulate self-understanding points beyond the ability to express such comprehension to the task of conception itself. The task is not just to *say* but to *conceive* who we are.[3] The examples of metaphors that have been used above imply that self-conception is dependent on language's plastic character. When we try to imagine who we are, we have no other recourse than to think of ourselves in relationship with other realities, often ones that are alien to ordinary descriptions of personhood. Self-understanding employs such comparison in conception as well as in articulation. Our minds produce pictures of ourselves; that is the only way we have of imagining ourselves as entities. Furthermore, we are likely to conceive those mental pictures with language. We think as well as speak in words. Our verbal expressions then are only the effort to share those imaginative pictures with others.

For at least these three reasons, self-understanding has more in common with poetry than with precise descriptive language. The latter will tell another very little. A congregation, for instance, might describe itself as having so many members, a budget of such and such, an average attendance at worship of so many, and a building located at such and such a place. Corporate self-understanding is never devoid of such descriptive information but goes much further. That same congregation might go on to say, "We are like a family!" Poetic language uses the richness of suggestion by putting words and phrases side-by-side to say something more than they might mean in other contexts.[4]

What can the church learn about its corporate self-understanding from the proposal that identity entails metaphorical language? Let's think, first, about metaphor, what it is and how it works. Then we can ask about the role of metaphor in self-understanding and how we create metaphors of this kind.

What Is Metaphor?

The question of the nature of metaphor has a long history in literary criticism, none of which concerns us here.[5] Tapping the resource of Paul Ricoeur's writings on the subject, we can define metaphor simply as the interaction among words and phrases in one particular context. Most important is that a metaphor juxtaposes two things, most often attributing an unusual quality to some common entity.[6] Suppose, for instance, someone says, "Jonesville Community Church is a recycling center!" We know the congregation, and we know what a recycling center is. But describing the congregation as a recycling center may surprise us, since we do not usually think of the church dealing with trash. Attributing the characteristics of a recycling center to a congregation provokes us to think about how a church could have such characteristics.

Metaphor puts some feature (in literary study, sometimes called the "vehicle") in relationship with another reality (the "tenor"). But the feature attributed to the reality under consideration is one not usually associated with it. In ordinary language we do not ascribe the characteristics of the one to the other. The relationship created by the use of an alien modifier expands the ordinary use of the words or expressions. Usually the subject or tenor (the Jonesville Community Church) is an ordinary one and the predicate or vehicle (a recycling center) one that is not commonly used of the subject. A metaphor, therefore, may be simply defined as assigning an odd characteristic to something in a way that violates the ordinary language of a particular community.[7]

> *For you shall go out in joy,*
> *and be led back in peace;*
> *the mountains and the hills before you*
> *shall burst into song,*
> *and all the trees of the field*
> *shall clap their hands. (Isa. 55:12)*

Mountains and hills sing; trees applaud! We know about mountains and hills, but we do not usually think of them as having voices and singing. We know about trees, but never thought of trees possessing hands, much less clapping them.

In some way or another, metaphor creates an interchange between two or more entities. Metaphor happens "from a kind of semantic proximity which suddenly obtains between terms in spite of their distance."[8] That exchange occurs out of the equation of the two realities (mountains and singing, trees and clapping hands) that are generally assumed to have nothing to do with one another. It is an equation that is obviously untrue in one sense. Trees do not have hands. But the invitation to think of how the equation is true, while at the same time false, sparks reflection. It violates the way we ordinarily use some word or expression.

Metaphors may come in at least three different shapes. Some are not true metaphors in the sense that they simply ask us to substitute ordinary language for the unusual words or phrases. I reduce the recycling metaphor to that kind when I say that it means Jonesville church makes people into new creations. Sometimes metaphorical comparison is easily translated back into ordinary language; that is, one may substitute a proposition for the metaphorical language and thereby capture its meaning.

Another kind of metaphor clues us that one thing is being compared with another by the inclusion of the words "like" or "as." "He is as restless as a long-tailed cat in a room filled with rocking chairs." The "as" asks us to form a mental picture of some sort. The simile, as this kind of metaphor is classically called, is still provocative and metaphorical in its use of language. For example, Jesus is frequently reported as saying, "the kingdom of heaven is like…" (e.g., Matt. 13:44, 45, and 47). What follows the "like" is every bit as stimulating as it would be had Jesus not used the comparative word "like," but Jesus tips off his listeners that they should be ready for the metaphor that follows. In doing so, he diminishes the surprise of associating something (e.g., a hidden treasure, a pearl, or a fishing net) with God's rule.[9] (See chapter 5.)

The third form of metaphor is direct and immediate in its creation of the extraordinary relationship of words and phrases (and the Isaiah quotation is a good example). Pure metaphor avails itself of the element of surprise, especially when it is found in a generally nonpoetic kind of work, and surprise is one of the ways metaphor works.

On the one hand, a metaphor is a creative and momentary event—an expression that happens and has its effect immediately. On the other hand, true metaphors have a richness in meaning that sustains them in our consciousness. They evoke a whole array of possible meanings and often stimulate a wider range of other metaphors. Because of this implicit power in some metaphors, many distinguish still another category of metaphors: root metaphors. These are profound relationships between words and phrases that have an unlimited number of interpretations. The potential exchange between the terms is so great that their impact endures in the imagination. Around these metaphorical relationships we can structure networks or clusters of other metaphors.[10] Christian life and faith entails a number of such root metaphors, such as the expression "God's people." Using the metaphor of possession, it pictures a peculiar relationship of a certain human group with their Creator (e.g., Ex. 3:7 and 1 Pet. 2:9–10). That metaphor spawned still others, most especially the language of God as parent and the community of faith as God's children (e.g., 1 John 3:2). The manner in which root metaphors work to evoke other images leads us to our second question.

How Does Metaphor Work?

First, a metaphor works by violating literal meaning. By literal we mean nothing more than the ordinary, dictionary meaning a word or phrase has. Our first impulse is to read sentences in terms of the descriptive and established sense of the words. "I am writing these words on a computer." When the sentence (or larger context) is absurd, however, we are forced to ask if something else is going on here. "I am writing these words on a Model T." The literal interpretation fails us, and we resort to a metaphorical reading—that computer of his must be old and obsolete. (Or, is it a priceless classic?)

Second, metaphor functions through the friction or tension it creates by means of the relationship between (or among) the terms. The friction begins with the strain created by the literal and metaphorical meanings. Trees clapping their hands: We imagine it literally and then metaphorically. The tension tightens as we consider the sense in which the relationship is true and false at the same time. Trees cannot clap; but maybe nature rejoices (creating another metaphor to understand the first). As a result of this quality, metaphors tend to create a view of reality that is tensive, that is, that has a both/and quality about it.[11] Christians are at the same time both saints and sinners.

Third, through this tension, metaphors create new meaning. When we read or hear a metaphor we try to construct some meaning out of it. We are deprived of a literal meaning by virtue of the strange relationship created by the metaphor, so we are compelled to think about another kind of meaning. What might it mean to say that mountains and hills sing in joy and the trees applaud when the people of Israel return to their homeland? Two things are important about the meaning metaphor creates. As we have said, it is new—something we had not thought before. However, that new meaning is not entirely clear. We make guesses at what the meaning might be, but it remains ambiguous.

A good metaphor never yields easily to our efforts to understand it. If we can simply substitute ordinary common words for the one strange word or expression the metaphor uses, then the metaphor is hardly effective. In the example given above you can easily replace "Model T" with "old and obsolete" and get the meaning of my words. (Even then, however, you have to wonder whether his computer is a classic.) True metaphor creates a relationship that cannot easily be translated into ordinary language. "You are the salt of the earth" (Matt. 5:13). We can paraphrase the possible meaning of the relationship between Christians and salt, but each of our paraphrases seems less than sufficient, and so we try again. To which quality of salt does the saying appeal? Our paraphrases go on and on without ever satisfactorily summarizing the exchange between Christians and salt. This is what writers mean when they say metaphor cannot be translated into literal terms or that one cannot satisfactorily substitute ordinary language for metaphorical language.[12]

Fourth, a metaphor's meaning is found, therefore, in something more fundamental. The provocative relationship articulates some fundamental experience and thereby opens a worldview. The meaning of religious metaphor especially is found in the peculiar vision of reality it suggests. That vision is essentially a matter of how we understand ourselves, our experience, and the whole realm of reality in which we find ourselves. So, a metaphor's meaning is found in something like a "being-in-the-world"—a way of perceiving and interpreting all experience. When Jesus speaks of Christians as "the salt of the earth," he opens the window shade a crack and allows us to peek through to glimpse a way of being on this earth. Metaphor is, therefore, world forming in the sense that it infiltrates our way of seeing and understanding.

Finally, we can say that metaphor works with the plastic quality of language to incite imagination. Metaphors arise from and appeal to the human capacity to visualize new possibilities. When a word or phrase can mean several things at the same time (trees, but trees with hands), it arouses that capacity for the possible. Ricoeur speaks of imagination as "the capacity for letting new worlds shape our understanding of ourselves."[13] Only by imagining the possibility of a new and different world can these strange metaphorical associations mean anything to us. If we shut down our imagining engines, metaphor becomes ridiculous tinkering with words.

This leads us to another kind of distinction among metaphors: "living" and "dead" metaphors. A true metaphor endlessly excites imagination to discern its meaning; they are inventions that provoke the reader or hearer to invent meaning.[14] They die (that is, lose their provocative quality) when we think we understand them and their meaning is regularized (e.g., put in the dictionary). For example, "the face of the clock" no longer invites imagination, since it is commonplace to speak of the clock as having a face. A living metaphor continues to shock us with its proximity of words and phrases. Once that association is no longer unusual and surprising, the metaphor dies. When a metaphorical expression becomes customary, it is no longer a true metaphor.

We seem to have a natural tendency to slay our metaphors and put them in the graveyard of the dictionary. This is particularly true of religious metaphors. We have, for instance, used the metaphor of "family" for the church so frequently and habitually that what once (in the origins of Christianity) was a surprising and provocative attribution of blood relationship with others in the faith community has become a cliché. The true metaphor makes us uneasy, since we cannot control it by saying this is what it means. In this sense, a metaphor threatens us, and we seek to contain it.[15] That uneasiness leads to our regularizing of certain metaphors so that they no longer bother us. We neutralize them by sucking out their creative and provocative blood. One question we will have to address later in our study is how we foster new metaphors of corporate self-understanding in the church without putting them to death! Can we really foster (i.e., manage) metaphors?

Metaphor and Self-understanding

Root metaphors provide the basic resources out of which a view of the world is fashioned. In technical language these are metaphors that create relationships among other metaphors, that is, networks of metaphors.[16] Such verbal relationships endlessly spawn still others and give birth to new understandings of our world and ourselves. Consequently they play the key role in shaping self-understanding.

A beginning point for thinking about such root metaphors is in daily language itself. Although their work is fraught with difficulties, George Lakoff and Mark Johnson studied the use of language in North America to lay bare our ordinary and daily conceptual systems. What they found was the pervasive presence of metaphorical language in everyday common speech. They define metaphor simply as "understanding and experiencing one kind of thing in terms of another."[17] They discovered that certain metaphors function as sources for much ordinary speech. Warfare, for instance, unfortunately permeates the daily speech of some.

When we say a person or project is "right on target," or an individual or idea "won the day," we are drawing on the basic metaphor of combat.

Ordinary, daily speech betrays the fact that certain rich and encompassing metaphors provide the framework within which we conceive and interpret all our experience. In a more fundamental sense than that which interests Lakoff and Johnson, we tend to grasp hold of broad metaphors that have to do with the way things are. One kind of example is the view captured in a popular song several decades ago, "We are dust in the wind." That metaphor expresses a fundamental vision of humans and the whole of reality. It provokes the image (or one paraphrase) of humans as tiny particles of valueless material pushed and pulled about by unpredictable and uncontrollable forces. Insofar as this image functions as a root metaphor, it gives rise to others and creates a system of metaphors, each of which furthers the same picture. For example, "puppets on the strings of an unknown puppeteer" or "mice in a maze." The organizing metaphor in this case expresses a view of life in the world and a lens through which experience may be interpreted.

Another such root metaphor creates a different image. "We are children of God." In this case, the metaphor suggests a peculiar relationship between humans and the Ultimate Reality. It transposes the human experience of parent-child into a cosmic view. Where such a basic metaphor dominates human consciousness, other metaphors cluster about it, including for instance the narrative metaphor we call the parable of the prodigal son (Luke 15:11–32). They may be infinitely expressed nonmetaphorically in propositions such as these: The Ultimate Reality accepts humans; humans are valuable; and the cosmos is friendly. Again, the organizing metaphor expresses a view of life in the world and a lens through which experience may be interpreted.

In either case, the root metaphor creates and expresses a human self-understanding (e.g., as either dust or precious children). Self-identity is constructed out of attributing some quality to our person—a quality that may or may not be literally appropriate either to humans or the whole of reality.

Lakoff and Johnson's conclusions about self-understanding are helpful:

> Understanding of ourselves is not unlike other forms of understanding—it comes out of our constant interactions with our physical, cultural and interpersonal environment ... Just as we seek out metaphors to highlight and make coherent what we have in common with someone else, so we seek out *personal* metaphors to highlight and make coherent our own pasts, our present activities, and our dreams, hopes, and goals as well. A large part of self-understanding is the search for appropriate personal metaphors that make sense of our lives.[18]

The authors go on to offer, among others, two suggestions for basic metaphors of self-understanding: "Developing an 'experiential flexibility' and "Engaging in an unending process of viewing your life through new alternative metaphors."[19]

Such root metaphors allow us to see something we had not seen before—to see in a new way. Ricoeur writes, "a metaphor may be seen as a model for changing our way of looking at things, of perceiving the world." Like poetic language it reveals "the deep structures of reality to which we are related ..." and creates "new possibilities of redescribing the world."[20] Consequently, metaphor does not "prompt learning, it causes it."[21]

Metaphors for self-identity allow us, then, to see ourselves in new ways—to grasp our own selves with clarity even though that clarity is enigmatic. Corporate self-understanding, like personal identity, is no less metaphorical. A root metaphor arises in a community and by it the community comes to conceive itself and its function. In the case of the church, however, the basic metaphor is intrinsic to Christian faith and the root metaphor of the church is part of that larger system of meaning we call doctrine or Christian faith. However, several reservations about what I am proposing must be addressed before we can proceed.

"Managing" Metaphors of Self-understanding

First among the issues we face is the question of the intentional creation or manipulation of metaphor. Can we just say, "Okay, we are going to create a metaphor by which we can understand ourselves as a church"? As we have observed, metaphors are creative and momentary events.[22] Their power is found in their surprise and suddenness. They are furthermore the result of flashes of creativity. Can we then manage the creation of metaphor? The answer has to be no. We cannot form a committee to invent a new metaphor for the church's identity any more than a committee can write a poem. The emergence of such new images for the church in a changing world is dependent on the creative imagination of its people.

We can, however, perhaps excite people to imagining. Reading poetry, for instance, always has the effect of fertilizing the reader's imagination for other metaphors. The church is called on to attend to metaphors for corporate self-understanding, but not necessarily to settle on one and then publish it in all the denominational educational and promotional literature. Metaphor births metaphor! The final chapter attempts to address this question more fully. To anticipate that discussion, one of the excitements for new metaphors for the church lies in a new appreciation of images used of the earliest Christian community in the New Testament. Those may not be precisely the ones we choose to embrace, but they will provoke new images within the body of Christ.

A second reservation comes to mind, for which we return to the mention of "dead" metaphor above. Is it not the case that by articulating new metaphors for our life together in the midst of a changing world we are endangering the very livelihood of those metaphors? Will our use of them to empower congregations to deal with change not simply wear them out?[23] Given our propensity for burying living metaphor in the closet of ordinary meaning, the answer in this case must be yes. The life-expectancy of a metaphor, however, depends on the richness of its meaning. The more provocative the metaphor is, the more struggle and search it requires, the more possible constructions of meaning it stimulates, the longer its life. The metaphors we offer to the church to aid it in its times of change need to be, therefore, as rich and as tantalizing as possible. How we employ such metaphors will also make a difference (see the final chapter).

Overuse kills metaphor, but not as much as closure kills it. Closing a metaphor is suggesting that we understand its meaning once and for all. Closure comes with words like "This is the true meaning of the words." Keeping a metaphor open has to do with how we read it and the confidence with which we claim to know what it says.[24] The metaphors for the church's identity in change will live only as long as we continue to struggle with their meaning.

Church Self-understanding and Change

This general discussion of metaphor and self-understanding, and especially the reservations about how we create and handle metaphor, readies us to investigate the church's metaphorical self-understanding in relation to change. But first it is necessary to introduce the word "image" and how it will be used throughout this study. In this discussion image means simply a mental picture evoked by language. Images are the imaginative visions excited by our encounter with language, through reading, hearing, or even seeing. If I should hear someone claim, "Our lives are dry deserts," my imagination immediately pictures the aridness and isolation of my experience. In a sense images are abbreviations of metaphors. An image is the "emerging meaning" resulting from metaphor.[25] So, images of the church are those mental pictures that arise from and represent metaphorical language about the community of Christian faith.

The goal of the following analysis is to scrutinize examples of current popular images of the church's self-understanding in the light of the reality of change. The thesis is that most of the current metaphors and their images of the church do not accommodate change either in the church itself or in its cultural setting. The images offered by theological studies is not the primary concern, but rather a sampling of those that seem operative in local congregations. Since this survey is necessarily selective, the discussion intends to invite readers to name images they know and hear most often and scrutinize them in a fashion similar to this analysis.

The images for the church selected for this discussion are of two kinds. The first are clusters of metaphors that in themselves clearly exclude and even oppose the reality of change. The second category includes some metaphors that might profitably account for change in culture and the church but which have been confined in their reference so as to exclude change. The following inquiry asks three questions about the images in both categories: What is the basic image, from what is it derived, and what are its implications for the capacity to deal with change?

Metaphors That Oppose Change

The first two images actually comprise one larger cluster of metaphors having to do with the stability of the church.

1. What Is the Basic Image? The basic image of the first group of metaphors at work in many concepts of the community of faith seems to be *haven*. In these cases the church is often spoken of as a safe-place, and the church is implicitly reduced to a location. But in some instances the community itself seems to serve as sanctuary. The haven is both a place of safety and a gathering of those with whom one can feel safe. The same dynamics function in images of the church as a place of *peace*. Such images articulate the profound need for security we all feel in an insecure and dangerous cultural environment. Consequently, many imagine the church as refuge from the world and its troubles.

From What Is the Image Derived? Obviously the images of the church as haven, refuge, and place of peace are rooted in scripture (e.g., Psalm 46) and are derived from one dimension of the Christian gospel. God graciously provides us haven and peace in relationship with our Creator (e.g., Ephesians 2:14). However, the biblical sense of peace and refuge has clearly been buried under more contemporary meanings of the words (e.g., the absence of turmoil and protection against trouble).

The Image and Change. Change is often one of the troubles from which the church is thought to secure us. When the images of the church as haven and peace prevail, we do not want changes to intrude themselves into the institution or its practices. Hence, relatively innocuous changes, such as the adoption of a new hymnal or the use of gender-inclusive language, disturb the stability. Worshipers may not want cultural changes even mentioned in the context of the service, since they have come to worship to escape such realities.

In our current cultural setting the images of peace and haven have prospered as expressions of the denial of change. For decades the eleven o'clock hour remained the most racially segregated period of time in our nation. The feminist movement may be progressing through all parts of our culture, but the church is sometimes the one place secure from such disruptions. Unwittingly the church's leadership has nurtured such images as haven and peace at the same time it tried to address the liberating qualities of the Christian message.

2. *What Is the Basic Image?* A second collection of images is closely related to the first. Part of the security we seek in the church (as either place or community) is stability, so the metaphors of the church as *fortress* and *rock* enjoy popularity. The church is protection and equilibrium.

From What Is the Image Derived? Like the first group of images, this second combination is transferred to the church from our image of God and/or Christ (e.g., Ps. 18:2). God is "a mighty fortress" and Christ a solid rock upon which we stand. Therefore, the church must logically be a fortress against the evils of the world and a rock protruding from an ocean of change and turmoil. Metaphors by their nature violate categories, so it should not surprise us that what we believe about God and Christ appears in our conceptions of the church. But in this case the violation of categories (i.e., God, therefore the church) fails to take seriously the radical otherness of the divine, not to mention the frailty of human nature.

The Image and Change. If God does not change (and that is the prevalent lay theology), then neither should the church change. The church is protection against transitions that threaten our identity and dissolve our presuppositions about reality. While the first collection of images perpetuates denial of the reality of change, this group directly opposes change. By implication change may even be identified with the evil from which the church protects us and the turmoil we escape by taking our stand on solid ground.

Conclusions. These two clusters of images do not in themselves misconstrue the gospel or our theologies of God and Christ, but they have become detrimental to a productive encounter with change. It is their use that makes them burdens to a church that must deal with cultural change and make changes within itself. The rehabilitation of these metaphors for our corporate identity requires putting them in another metaphorical context (network) that is more realistic about and dialogically engaged with change. Another way of saying this is that these images lack the both/and quality of true metaphor. Their reformation requires that they be set in tension (paradoxical relationship) with other images that picture the church immersed in change.

Metaphors Restricted to Exclude Change

The second cluster of images is those which in themselves may imply change but which have been narrowed in ways that disregard change. Transition might be integral to these images when they are fully embraced, at least in our culture, but they have suffered from constraints that isolate them from change.

1. *What Is the Basic Image?* The first group of images is *familial*. "The family," "sisters and brothers in Christ," and "kinship" emerge from this basic vision of the community of faith. In actual practice these images often express a sense of comfort people feel with one another within the church. When a congregation characterizes itself as a family, more often than not it means the group shares enough values with one another that a sense of ease obtains among them. For instance, a family-oriented congregation of which I was a member seemed to accept a gay member, while in point of fact they simply pretended that he was one of them and denied his homosexuality. Hence, they preserved the notion that they were a group of like-minded people, that is, a family.

From What Is the Image Derived? The metaphor of believers as family is deeply rooted in the familial language of scripture itself, beginning with language used of the people of Israel (e.g., Hos. 11:1–3). The image is found running throughout both testaments, but the New Testament emphasizes it with language of adoption as children of God (e.g., Gal. 4:5). It roots in the image of God as parent, one of the many metaphors for God's relation with humanity captured most forcefully in Jesus' speaking of God as *Abba*. That image spills over into relations among believers as siblings and the whole community as family. The cluster of images is solidly biblical and profoundly theological.

The Image and Change. The metaphor of the community as family under God's parenthood and Christ as our brother suffers a number of unfortunate implications for the church today. Many of these implications are due to an emerging societal understanding of the family. The metaphor of the church as a family suffers from two sociological developments and their implications. The first development is that family is increasingly narrowly defined as husband, wife, and children. The second is that today's nuclear family is an exclusive entity without provisions for including others. Single people, couples without children, and gay and lesbian unions all fall beyond the boundaries of the popular cultural conception of family. The problem in this case is not with the basic biblical imagery but with the way in which the category of family is understood in our culture.

More to the point, in their use the familial images of the church have tended to be systematically restricted. For instance, if the church is a family, can it—like the families we know—be dysfunctional? Seldom, if ever, will we hear the metaphor used in terms of a capacity for abuse and hostility or for potentially damaging as well as healing relationships. The metaphor's restricted reference that interests us the most is the exclusion of any sense of growth, transition, or change. The family invariably changes, no matter what its precise makeup. As family members change, so too does the family itself. Children grow up, go off to college, leave home; parents age, take new jobs, move, retire; aged grandparents move in and grown children back in. Today the real family is constantly in transition.[26] Yet when the family is used metaphorically of the church, it is most often hardened into an unchanging entity without reference to transition. Some idyllic stage in the life of a family is the sole reference to which the church is compared. Theoretically we could use the family metaphor in its full richness to speak of the church constantly in transition. Congregations experience the same kind of transitions experienced in families today. But that dimension of the family experience has been truncated from the familial image of the church. Much of the same thing has happened to the second basic image.

2. *What Is the Basic Image?* The church as Christ's own body is both the basic and most common image. From it arises less frequent images such as "parts of the body."

From What Is the Image Derived? Pauline thought is the root of this image. It is impossible to know if Paul consciously thought of his language as metaphorical or if he intended it as a literal description of how Christ was present in the world. But the language of passages in 1 Corinthians 12, Romans 12, Ephesians 1:23, Colossians 1:18–19, as well as other passages by implication (e.g., 1 Cor. 10:16–17 and 11:27–29), clearly functions metaphorically. The entity of the human body is provocatively set in relationship to the church. Theological reflection on incarnation has further enriched the imagery. The image is solidly biblical and theologically profound.

The Image and Change. Once again, an odd sort of delimiting of the metaphor has occurred. Granted Paul does not explicitly include the dimension of bodily change in his original metaphor. However, he does speak of "building up (*oikodomeo*) the church" (1 Cor. 14:12). The author of Ephesians, who was either Paul or one of his disciples, uses the phrase "building up the body of Christ" (Eph. 4:12—see chapter 4). Changes in the body of Christ are not foreign to Pauline thought. When the image is viewed in its broader New Testament context, growth and maturation are clearly one of the components of the body of Christ.

Moreover, contemporary understandings of the human body make it impossible to ignore the implication of change when visualizing the church as Christ's physical embodiment. We know that the human body is in a constant state of change and that even our material composition as bodies is entirely new over time. It seems evident that the contemporary church has been hesitant to use the metaphor both in terms of what we now know about the body and how the New Testament speaks of the church as Christ's body. That hesitancy speaks volumes about the church's uneasiness with conceiving of itself as a community in constant and endless transition.

Conclusion. With these two groups of images for the church we witness several important facts. The first is that metaphors change as their cultural reference changes. Metaphorical language draws a characteristic from one realm of experience to set it in dialogue with another reality. But when that characteristic undergoes change as part of culture, the metaphor, too, changes. The family structures of biblical times are no longer identical with those of our time; our understanding of the human body is not the same as Paul's. Cultural changes affect our basic metaphors, even making some of them obsolete. When cultural changes influence our metaphors, we have a number of options. We may adapt them to correspond to the contemporary situation and understanding, abandon them, or restrict their meaning. The images of family and the body for the church require reinterpretation, if they are to remain effective and empowering for change.

Second, in the limitations imposed on the images of family and body we witness our failure of courage to confront change. Responsibility for the restriction of meaning to be constructed from these two metaphors falls to the whole church but necessarily especially to its leadership. In far too many cases we have not wanted to imagine ourselves as a family or a body in transition for fear of opening the floodgates of change and being swept away in the wake. The church needs new imaging as a changing entity in a changing culture, but the problem goes deeper. We have not availed ourselves of the full potential of our current images to address change.

Toward New Self-understanding

Whether the answer lies in rehabilitating current images of the church or appropriating fresh ones, one can hardly deny that the church's current self-understanding does not equip us to engage change in creative dialogue. Contemporary metaphors either exclude change entirely or have been interpreted with the same result. Our situation calls for new corporate self-understanding, for as a church we can no longer afford to deny the dynamic dimension of the body of Christ or the radical state of transition in our culture. Suzette Haden Elgin rightly claims, "I believe [metaphors] are the *only efficient* way to bring about real change in human attitudes."[27] I propose two steps we can take toward a new self-understanding.

Tension-filled Images

Metaphor is the language with which we conceive and articulate corporate as well as personal self-understanding. One feature of metaphorical language is peculiarly important in this process: Metaphors are inherently filled with tension. The tension resides initially in the relationship created by juxtaposing two terms or phrases. The interpretation of metaphorical language also involves tension: First in the opposition of literal and metaphorical meanings and second in the ambiguity created by the exchange between the entities. That ambiguity, as we have said, leaves us searching for the meaning of a metaphorical relationship.[28]

In several ways the tension within metaphor and its interpretation parallels the tension inherent in change and the church. The church must live within a polarity between changing with culture and resisting change for the sake of its tradition (see chapter 1). Our dilemma is that the church does change and must change, but at the same time we claim that there is something inherently unchanging in the basic Christian message. Tradition and cultural adaptation apply pressure in opposite directions. Metaphorical language gains its power through the strain between the "is" and the "is not" of the juxtaposing of words and phrases. The images of the church's identity need therefore to capitalize on both the "is" and the "is not" character of true metaphors.[29] Every metaphor hints at similarity while it shocks us with its dissimilarity. Metaphors of the church in change are capable of stressing both the transitional character of the community of faith and its continuity with its heritage at the same time.

Another benefit of metaphorical images for the church has to do with a similar tension within Christians themselves: The sense in which we are both *in* the world but not *of* the world (see 1 John 4:4–6). Our historical location is in a specific cultural environment that forms us from our births. Our ultimate origin and destination, however, is from another realm, and we seek the influence of that transcendent realm on who we are. Again, the tension between the two might be captured in the tension between the two components of metaphor. Can we construct metaphors that recognize the reality of life in a culture and at the same time claim roots that are beyond that culture? We are both like and unlike our culture, and any pretense to be otherwise is either unrealistic or unfaithful.

Finally, and perhaps most important, is that the tension inherent in metaphor creates a view of reality that is itself filled with tension.[30] Metaphor sustains the tensive quality of existence we all know and experience. As there is an intrinsic "back pressure"[31] in the metaphorical relationship, there is a similar pressure in reality itself. Knowing this, Christians have long resorted to paradox to speak what they apprehend to be true—statements which are logically contradictory but which when taken together speak the truth of experience. For example, the church declares that Christ was both truly human and at the same time truly divine (see the Athanasian Creed). Metaphor is the linguistic equivalent of a paradoxical comprehension of reality and thus is the nature of the language of faith.

The "method of metaphor" is then the most promising and appropriate means by which we can both finesse the delicate situation in which the church and Christians find themselves and discover language with which to speak our faith. But as Christians we do not create metaphors out of nothing or even out of culture alone.

New Testament Images

If scripture is in some way or another still authoritative for our Christian understanding, the basic source of metaphors of corporate self-understanding is the Bible.[32] We cannot, of course, simply parrot biblical language. To do so denies our own cultural identity and isolates us from our culture as a sect. The imagery of scripture needs cultural translation even as the early texts require translation from their original language into ours.[33] Translations of those pictures that the earliest groups of God's people fashioned for themselves remain the first and primary resource for images of our corporate identity. Those biblical images can be re-expressed in language that captures contemporary experience as well as elucidates churchly identity. Biblical language provokes contemporary images, much the way poetic metaphor stimulates other metaphorical language. The richness of New Testament images of the church stirs new and contemporary images for our self-understanding.

The next three chapters propose translations of three New Testament metaphors for the church's self-understanding: (1) "on the way," (2) "home and homing," and (3) "stumbling in the light." With these three images (or clusters of images) we will construct a single metaphorical sentence for who we are as a church: "The church is a community of faith on the way home, stumbling in the light." Both in its three component parts and as a whole, the impact of the biblical language points us toward a new corporate self-identity that includes and takes change seriously. Furthermore, this self-identity employs the method of metaphor, has the tensional quality of such language, and at the same time is grounded in the biblical witness.

CHAPTER THREE

"On the Way"

"The church is a community of faith on the way."

Each of the four gospels includes early episodes in which Jesus calls persons to "follow" him (Matt. 4:18–22; Mark 1:16–20; Luke 5:27–28; and John 1:35–43). Luke further informs us of a small group that traveled with Jesus as he went from village to village (Luke 8:1–3). For good reason "following" the Galilean preacher-healer comes to symbolize discipleship (e.g., Mark 2:15). The image of such following naturally leads to the conception of the path the first believers took in accompanying Jesus. That path is represented in the word "way," an expression that in itself came to represent Christian life and faith. Mark 10:52 is a good example. Jesus is on his way to Jerusalem (Mark 10:32) when he meets and heals blind Bartimaeus. The narrator then describes Bartimaeus' actions: "Immediately he regained his sight and followed (Jesus) *on the way.*" The Gospel of John expands and modifies that reference to discipleship with Jesus' claim that he himself is the "way" (John 14:6).[1]

Acts first uses "the Way" (in Greek, *hodos*) to speak of Christians in 9:2 and then repeats that title at least five more times (19:9, 23; 22:4; 24:14, 22). Most often those who are not believers use the expression to refer to Christians, or its use entails the controversy Christians cause. By implication "the way" suggests that the path of the church in the first century was a difficult one. The word is common in the Old Testament (in Hebrew, *derek*), where it refers to lifestyle. It occurs sometimes to speak of the way of life of those who are evil or disobedient (e.g., Ps. 1:1; Prov. 1:31) and sometimes of those who are faithful to God, that is, "the way of the Lord" (e.g., Ps. 86:11; Isa. 35:8). The word then is wealthy with profound and biblical innuendoes.[2]

This chapter proposes that the gospels portray a Christian community journeying "on the way" with Jesus into a new future and that this image is fundamental to what it means to be the church. However, before beginning investigations of texts related to this image, it is necessary to make some observations about the method of interpreting scripture for the purposes of this study. The effort will be to examine the biblical text and pose a reading for the contemporary church. There will be no pretense of unearthing the original intention of the authors of the texts. Contemporary movements in biblical interpretation have shown that any such effort to do so is fraught with difficulties.[3] We can never know exactly what any author intended with the words we have in the ancient text. The text is itself rich with possibilities for the church, some of which may exceed whatever it was the author intended. True, we must use every bit of historical information we have to understand the original setting of any text and remain consistent with the sense of any biblical passage, but the historical information is not abundant enough for us to make absolute claims that this or that interpretation is the "true reading" of any text. What we seek is a reading that is consistent with the possibilities of the language of the text.

Such a development in the community of scholarship does not surprise those of us in the church, for we have always claimed that the Bible's relevance for our life together exceeds whatever might have been the original purpose of its authors. The apostle Paul, for instance, would be surprised to learn that his occasional letters to budding Christian churches throughout the Roman Empire in the first century continue to be read in terms of their message for the church two thousand years later! So, our efforts to attend to the suggestions of the text for Christian communities facing a crisis of change are consistent with contemporary biblical interpretation, but more importantly with the classical role of the scripture in the church.[4]

The church's reading of the image of disciples traveling a way has evoked the journey metaphor for Christian life and faith. That metaphor has become a classic theme in Christian spirituality that continues even today.[5] Because it is so prominent in our heritage and in current reflections on Christian spirituality, our study of the biblical theme "on the way" begins with an assessment of the image of journey, sojourn, or pilgrimage. After that the chapter focuses on the journey theme found in the Gospel of Luke and Acts. A conclusion pulls the Lukan fragments on this theme together around the image of way and offers an analysis of its potential for helping the church understand itself in relationship to change.

The Classic Image of Christian Journey

How, if at all, does the image "on the way" take us beyond the older and well-worn metaphor of Christian life as a journey, sojourn, or pilgrimage? Harriet Crabtree has critically analyzed the metaphor of pilgrimage in terms of its adequacies for contemporary Christian life. These are some of her results.

Problems and Potentials in the Metaphor

Crabtree correctly isolates three tensions or paradoxes the metaphor of journey might sustain. The first of these is between traditional patterns of living and the living word of God. On the one hand, the journey theme values the church's rich heritage but, on the other hand, invites openness to new understandings of the divine will. The second tension is between the individual and the community. The metaphor of journey has tended to emphasize the individual at the expense of the community. However, Crabtree observes, "In fact, the metaphor lends itself very well to this stress on community. Most actual pilgrims have never gone alone."

The third way in which such metaphors as journey, sojourn, or pilgrimage tend to pull in two directions at once has to do with the present and the future. Crabtree thinks that they tend to emphasize the "not yet" to the minimization of "attachment and relations."[6] She says the metaphor is essentially masculine in that it stresses the renunciation of human relationships. There is also often a preoccupation with the goal of the journey in the use of this image. Still, the tension between individual life and social justice has been restored in most contemporary uses of the images. Nonetheless, Crabtree prefers the image of the Christian life as a "destinationless 'walk'" that is less focused on the goal of the journey.[7] Furthermore, "If God is understood to be traveling … then the value of the present, in which God is moving with us, is more firmly established."[8] Crabtree also suggests the image's usefulness depends in large measure on the biblical material on which it is based, since there is a great diversity of biblical journeys.

With these reservations in mind, Crabtree concludes:

> We need to develop the metaphor with a greater eye to its communal dimension and to that aspect of the creator God which leads us to affirm the goodness of the created order. We need also to take seriously the idea of the Pilgrim God who works with us to *create* the destination, as well as draw us close.[9]

Crabtree believes there are two specific theological challenges in an assessment of any of our metaphors: Evaluating the truthfulness and the usefulness of the images. To meet the criterion of truthfulness requires keeping any metaphor in relation with others (or, as I would argue, in tension with other metaphors). About the second requirement she observes that any new images "will take a long time to take root." Still, she concludes, "it is only by beginning new traditions of symbolization that one opens up the possibility for change."[10]

Reframing the Image of Journey

Can we begin new traditions of images, avoid the dangers of the journey theme Crabtree has pointed out, and still preserve its heritage? Perhaps reworking the journey theme within the framework of "on the way" responds to that question and "opens up the possibility for change." The restudy of the Lukan travel materials in the gospel and Acts may provide fresh information that corrects the weaknesses of the pilgrimage metaphor and strengthens its potential as a communal image.

The following study of the Lukan journey theme suggests how being the church on the way requires and enhances relationships, an engagement with the world in matters of social well-being, and participation in the community. Moreover, Luke-Acts accents a subplot of continual discovery in its use of the way imagery. Of course, all four gospels suggest the element of discovery in following Jesus (e.g., John 1:43–51), but Luke and Acts seem to underscore such revelations. The beginnings of the Christian community were in the surprises it experienced in following Jesus and later the Spirit. These surprises are essential to an understanding of the metaphor of the way.

Still another issue is involved in the reframing of the journey motif with the image of the way. The Lukan portrayal of the journey theme focuses on Jerusalem; it is the hinge on which the way swings. The Gospel of Luke pictures Jesus' journey to Jerusalem where he fulfills his divine destiny. The Acts of the Apostles describes the earliest Christians' movement out from Jerusalem into the Greco-Roman world. Luke honors Jerusalem's ancient role as God's own city, even though the city is compromised by human sin and pride. It is the site of Jesus' unjust death, and later of Stephen's (Acts 7:54–60). So, the city's role is never that of the ideal home we find in Hebrews and Revelation (see chapter 4), but it is the point of the church's beginnings. The Lukan image of Jerusalem is the point at which the pilgrim God begins the journey into the whole world. In Christ, God returns to Jerusalem, desolated as it may be, and from there moves "to the ends of the earth" (Acts 1:8).

The Journey Theme in the Gospel of Luke

Introduction

Luke and Acts. Most biblical students today agree that the Gospel of Luke and its canonical companion piece, the Acts of the Apostles, were written, if not by the same author, at least by early Christians from the same community. Each is read most richly in continual reference to the other, so that one may safely speak of their comprising a two-volume set on the origins of Christianity.[11] The Gospel of Luke and the Acts are, to be sure, different in literary genre. The first follows the literary form of Mark and the second a literary form unique in the New Testament but not in the Greco-Roman world.[12]

Notwithstanding the literary distinctiveness of each of these two documents, in both of them we find the journey theme. That theme doubtless arises from Luke's commitment to the continuity between the Old Testament and the early Christian movement. Two of the foundational characters of the Hebrew scriptures, Abraham and Moses, both engage in adventuresome journeys in obedience to God. For instance, Luke is the only evangelist who claims that the exodus is central to Jesus' transfiguration (Luke 9:31, where the NRSV translates *exodos*, "departure"). In the third gospel Jesus' journey to Jerusalem replicates Israel's desert sojourn in Canaan, much as his temptation in the wilderness replicates the people's experience in the wilderness of their pilgrimage (Luke 4:1–13).

Our inquiry begins with the Gospel of Luke and then only briefly shows how the theme of travel is carried through into the Acts story. The centrality of journey for the church represented in Acts, however, casts its shadow back into the Gospel of Luke, suggesting that the disciples' journey with Jesus is representative of the whole church's life together.

The Lukan Travel Section. Scholars have long puzzled over the fact that at Luke 9:51 Jesus "set his face to go to Jerusalem" and that the journey to Jerusalem continues through 19:27. The intervening contents of the gospel are framed within the trip, but the destination is mentioned only twice more in the passage (13:22 and 17:11) before Jesus and his followers reach Jerusalem. Moreover, these chapters hardly suggest simple geographical movement. Little is said about the itinerary Jesus and his band followed, and by 17:11 they are still "between Samaria and Galilee."[13] The section has been labeled the "Large Interpolation," since most of its material is not found in Mark. Some have thought that the evangelist contrived the travel narrative only as a device for including stories and teachings not contained within Mark's simple structure (that is, stories and teachings drawn from the Q sayings source and from Luke's special sources). If the third evangelist used Mark's gospel as the pattern of the story, why does the Lukan story depart so radically at this point from the Markan framework? This is especially puzzling, since up to 9:51 Luke seems to have followed that framework for much of the Jesus story. Numerous theories have been offered, including the suggestion that the evangelist patterns the contents of these chapters after Deuteronomy 1–26.[14]

At the level of the narrative itself this section of the Gospel of Luke accomplishes at least two things. First, it heightens the suspense of the narrative.[15] The first two passion announcements are narrated in 9:22 and 44. So, we know Jesus' destiny, but the narrative holds us in anticipation as it moves through the ten chapters of this long travel section. Second—and most important for this study—by means of this large section of material the gospel puts the journey theme front stage. In doing so, these chapters anticipate the church's travel in the Acts story. But they also suggest that Christian discipleship is itself journey. Following Jesus entails travel, both of a geographical and of a more existential kind (i.e., spiritual).

The journey design functions metaphorically rather than geographically.[16] The text conjures images of a group following Jesus on a journey that is concerned more with insight and discovery than with ground covered. This view of the travel section of Luke is bolstered by a number of features of the whole gospel and the Acts. (The evidence of Acts will occupy our attention later in this chapter.)

From its beginning the gospel's narrative alerts readers that journeys are going to play an important role in the plot. There's a whole lot of traveling going on throughout the gospel's story. Already in chapter 1 Mary journeys to an unnamed village in Judah to meet Elizabeth. Chapter 2 begins with a journey from Nazareth to Bethlehem and back again and concludes with another trip—this one from Nazareth to and back from Jerusalem. With such an introduction to journeying, the narrator tells us of Jesus' excursions. He is constantly on the move, coming and going to this place or another, all in the region of Galilee (e.g., Luke 7:1–11, from Capernaum to Nain). Then at the heart of the plot, following on the heels of the passion predictions and the transfiguration story in chapter 9, Jesus sets out on the journey to Jerusalem. His movement to Jerusalem reminds us of the journey of the holy family in chapter 2. Thus the evangelist frames the whole of the Jesus story with journeys to Jerusalem, like bookends supporting the narrative at its beginning and end. The story's climax comes at the conclusion of this journey, and Jesus' last journey in the Gospel of Luke is his ascension (24:50–53).

Others are also sent on journeys because of Jesus: John sends his disciples to Jesus in chapter 7; Jesus sends the twelve out in chapter 9 and the 70 (or 72) in chapter 10. Travel is featured even in Jesus' teachings in the Gospel of Luke. Of Jesus' parables found only in this gospel, three entail trips: the good Samaritan (10:25–37), the friend at night (11:5–8), and the prodigal son (15:11–32). Note that all three are found in the travel narrative chapters of the gospel. Jesus tells stories about traveling in the midst of his journey. Not incidentally, the story of the risen Christ's appearance to two disciples on the road to Emmaus (24:13–35) is also a narrative unique to Luke among the gospels.

Surprises on the Way

In the narrative world of the third gospel, journeying is of vital importance, but what happens to Jesus' followers in the midst of this prolonged journey to Jerusalem? That may tell us more about the Lukan journey motif than the territory traversed. A simple answer to the question is that the community of followers experience one surprise after another. The world of the third gospel is filled not only with travel but also with surprising reversals discovered amid those travels with Jesus.[17]

Those important stories of births in chapters 1 and 2 alert the readers early on to the reversal feature of Luke's narrative world. Mary's song of praise (the famous Magnificat, Luke 1:46–55) powerfully rehearses God's activity in inverting human conditions (e.g., filling the hungry with good things, and sending the rich away empty—1:53). Not kings or priests, but a bunch of lowly shepherds are the first to receive the news of the birth of this wondrous child and what that means for the world (2:8–20). Then old Simeon declares that this child would occasion the fall and rising of many in Israel (2:34). In his sermon in the synagogue at Nazareth (Luke 4:18–21), Jesus announces that his ministry would reverse the fortunes of many: good news to the poor, release of the captives, sight for the blind, and freedom for the oppressed. The acts and words of Jesus' ministry, then, are filled with surprising changes—the poor are blessed, the ill and afflicted healed, and the outcasts befriended. But the gospel's conclusion brings the grand reversal. An innocent man is put to death and buried in a tomb, but then God raises him, and he appears to his followers.

In the Gospel of Luke the divine determination entails turning everything upside down. The normal course of events, the normal expectations of the real historical world in which the story is set (Luke 1:1–4) are disturbed. The fortunes of mighty rulers and institutions are altered. This is a world filled with surprising reversals for all the characters in the story, not least of all those who follow Jesus. We are not surprised, then, to learn how Jesus' followers experienced reversals while traveling with their teacher. Jesus himself affords them an example of surprising reversal in following God on the way. In the story of the healing of the centurion's servant (Luke 1:1–10), Luke tells us that Jesus is surprised (the Greek word is *thaumazen*, meaning to wonder, marvel or be astonished) at the Gentile's faith (Luke 7:9). (See Mark 7:24–30; Matt. 15:21–28 for a comparable story.) Jesus is amazed to find faith among the Gentiles. God is reversing their conditions as well as the Jews'. (The early church would later replicate such a similar surprise.) With Jesus as the model for discerning God's astonishing work, in the context of journey, the text shows how the nascent faith community faced change and transformation of identity.

The Lukan travel narrative is ripe with surprising reversals. We have time to isolate only four of them on the way to Jerusalem. Each of them is really only one side of the single gem of the reversal God causes in Christ.

The Unfaithful Are Faithful. The journey to Jerusalem has hardly begun when the disciples learn a serious lesson. A Samaritan village rejects Jesus, and the disciples want it burned to the ground, but he rebukes their vengeful wish (9:52–56).[18] That story only scratches the surface. Later Jesus tells the story of the Samaritan who aided a needy traveler after a priest and a Levite had ignored him. The issue is "who is my neighbor?" (10:29 and 36). The parable surprises the journeyers and all who hear it. A detested and ostracized Samaritan is pictured as the one who serves as a neighbor to the needy (10:30–37). No self-respecting Jew of the time would suppose an unfaithful Samaritan capable of faithfulness, much less of serving as the hero in a rabbi's story.

Another story imprints the same lesson on the disciples' minds and hearts. Jesus heals a group of ten lepers but only one returns to express his gratitude (17:11–19). As the healed man prostrates himself at Jesus' feet, the narrator sneaks in a startling fact: "And he was a Samaritan" (17:16). A Samaritan capable of a healing and saving faith! Jesus is reversing all the disciples' cherished social stereotypes and prejudices. They learn an openness to finding faithfulness among those least expected to exhibit it. Jesus does the same thing with his parable of the Pharisee and the tax collector (18:9–14). Those who participated in the oppression of the common people by gathering taxes were national turncoats. They were also religious sinners, making themselves unclean through dealings with Gentiles, but in this shocking story one of them displays a righteousness in contrast to that of a religious leader. The tax collector knows that the lowest place before God is the highest (see below).

The tendency to draw boundaries between the faithful and the unfaithful is intrinsic to nearly every religious movement. In all of the gospels, including this portion of Luke (e.g., 11:37–54; 12:1–3; and 16:15), Jesus sharply assaults the religious establishment of his day. However, his attack is at least in part against every effort to define faithfulness and then exclude all those who fall outside the definition. A church that is on the way with Jesus soon learns that the unfaithful may indeed be the faithful.

The Needy Are Blessed. The second reversal is simply another side of the first, since the human condition of need was understood in Jesus' culture to be evidence of sin (i.e., unfaithfulness). That understanding roots in a stream of Old Testament thought, namely, that faithfulness is rewarded in this life with well-being and success (e.g., Job's insistence that he does not deserve his dire condition).[19] Therefore, to claim that the needy are blessed reverses ordinary assumptions about them. The radical reversal of the needy echoes words Jesus' followers have heard before; he often speaks of the poor (e.g., 6:20). In Luke's Gospel, Jesus' whole ministry focuses on his compassion for the needy[20] (e.g., 4:16–21), so this important theme in the travel narrative does not catch us readers entirely unprepared.

Two healing stories strike us with their similarities. Jesus heals a crippled woman on the Sabbath, and the religious leaders charge him with violation of the Sabbath commandment against work. He responds that everyone cares for their livestock on the Sabbath, and this woman ("a daughter of Abraham") is at least as valuable as livestock (13:10–17). The healing of a man with dropsy is similar. Human need is more important than faithfulness to the Sabbath commandment (14:1–6). Surely his followers are among those who rejoice to hear such words (13:17), but just as surely they must wonder at the radical reversal of religious life their leader espouses.

The charge that Jesus "welcomes sinners and eats with them" (15:2) illumines another dimension of Jesus' associations with the needy outcasts of his day. "Sinners" includes those who suffered from human affliction, else why would they be in that condition? (See John 9:1–2) Their condition, moreover, was contagious and to eat with them put one in danger of contracting their plight.[21] To the surprise of the established religion of the day, Jesus concentrated his ministry on those who were despised. In Luke that concentration is sometimes expressed as God's concern for the "lost." Jesus declares that his mission is "to seek out and to save the lost" (19:10). Chapter 15 contains three parables having to do with finding the lost and the divine joy over their restoration.

Like most Jews of the time, Jesus' traveling companions believe that human tragedy results from sin. So his denial that one can measure the degree of sin by the extent of tragic occurrences catches them off guard (13:1–5). Instead of affirming the relationship between sin and suffering, Jesus issues a call to repentance without which one will perish. But on the heels of that declaration of strict divine justice he tells a parable of patience. An unproductive fig tree is granted a reprieve for another year while it is nurtured with fertilizer (13:6–9). Justice and patience are posed side by side.

The heart of this radical reversal of the state of the needy, however, is found in Jesus' teachings about the poor and the use of wealth. One parable warns of the seductive dangers of wealth (12:16–21), and Jesus claims that seeking God's reign provides all that is necessary (12:31). The story of the rich man and Lazarus still more poignantly makes much the same point (16:19–31). To have eternal life requires that those who have give to those who do not have (18:22). Jesus responds to a dinner invitation by insisting that one should invite "the poor, the crippled, the lame, and the blind" to dinner (14:12–14). Then he tells a story of an unnamed person who threw a big dinner party, but all the invited guests made excuses for not coming. The host then orders that the servants go out and bring in "the poor, the crippled, the blind, and the lame" for the dinner (14:15–24). His listeners are forced to consider God's radical reversal of the conditions of the needy.[22]

The blessedness of the needy clashes with any attempt to identify God's blessing with good health or material prosperity. That ancient tendency is liable to creep up on a church that is not on the way with its Christ. (See Luke's beatitudes and parallel "woes"—6:20–26.)

The Highest Place Is the Lowest. This shocking and almost nonsensical reversal is close to the previous one. In the wake of Jesus' prediction of his passion (9:43–45), the disciples squabble over which of them is the greatest. With a child Jesus tries to show them a different kind of greatness. He declares in that context "the least among all of you is the greatest" (9:46–48). Now Jesus treats his followers to a series of teachings to implant this reversal in their lives.

A parable of taking the "lowest place" at a wedding banquet puts the point in a narrative form. To get their attention Jesus structures the story in terms of honor and shame. Just to make sure his message is clear, he expresses it in an admonition at the conclusion of the story: "All who exalt themselves will be humbled, and those who humble themselves will be exalted" (14:7–11). The saying duplicates the conclusion to the story of the Pharisee and tax collector mentioned above (18:14).

The honor of the lowest position drills to the core of human life. A similar penetration results from another of Jesus' declarations: "Those who try to make their life secure will lose it, but those who lose their life will keep it" (17:33).[23] Such a reversal of personal and cultural standards is difficult to grasp, for it remains shrouded in the mystery of the cross itself. Jesus is on his way to Jerusalem, where he himself will lose his life to keep it. In the process he tries to convince those of us who travel that route with him of the meaning of surrendering all security to gain real life.

The Powerless Are Powerful. This last theme speaks to the question of the church's potential for traveling with Jesus in service of the world. Where within the community is the power to transcend our culture's stereotypes to see faithfulness in the unfaithful, to enact God's blessing of the needy, to take our station in the lowest position, and to share God's compassion to find the lost?

The claim that the powerless are powerful is anchored, first of all, in Christ's portrayal of power. As he pictures it, Christian power has nothing to do with worldly power (see 9:46–48) nor with station, as the whole story of Jesus demonstrates. The central feature of such power is the willingness to surrender life in service of others, as Christ does through his ministry and will do supremely in going to the cross. Therefore, the empowerment of the powerless is founded exclusively in Jesus' own authority.

In the travel narrative that authority is given to Jesus' followers as in Acts it is given to the church through the Spirit (Luke 24:49 and Acts 1:8). In Luke 9 Jesus empowers and sends out the twelve to preach and heal (9:1–6). In the very next chapter a wider circle is commissioned. Jesus sends seventy (or seventy-two, depending on which ancient text is taken as authority) of his followers to villages he wishes to visit (10:1–16). They return exuberant over the fact that they were empowered to command demons. They have discovered that their alignment with Jesus and his mission invests their words with new authority (10:17). Jesus affirms their new insight with the remarkable words of 10:18–20: "I watched Satan fall from heaven, like a flash of lightning. See, I have given you authority (or power—*exousia*) to tread on snakes and scorpions, and over all the power (*dynamis*) of the enemy ..." Their ministry is possible because of Christ's gift to them, and with it they are dethroning the evil powers of the world. Mere mortals participate in God's reclamation of creation!

That empowering story comes early in the Lukan travel narrative. The parable of the pounds (19:11–27) concludes the travel section by elaborating the empowerment of the powerless. Upon his departure, a nobleman entrusts a portion of his wealth to ten of his servants. Each receives a single pound and then proceeds to care for it. When the nobleman returns, he finds that two servants have each invested their pounds and have made additional sums for their master. A third, however, was fearful of his master and did nothing more than preserve the gift with which he was entrusted. (See the comparable parable in Matt. 25:14–30 and the very different one in Mark 13:34.)

Obviously the parable of the pounds is complicated and rich with suggestion. But when it is linked with the authorization of followers in chapter 10, it yields even more interesting possibilities. In this context the parable invites us to think about God's entrusting the church with power and our willingness to venture the risk of using that power in the service of others. The fearful servant is instructive for a church in a season of change. Can we accept the gift with which God entrusts us and have the courage to use it in ways that further the divine presence in our world? Or, shall we bury our portion of the authority of Christ in the ground in fear of misusing God's trust? On the way with Christ we find ourselves empowered and sent in mission to the world.

Conclusions

There is still another journey in the gospel that merits a brief note. Two disciples are journeying to Emmaus and on the way meet a stranger who eventually proves to be their risen Master (24:13–35). To their surprise the resurrected Christ appears to them as an ordinary, if learned, traveler. We learn to be sensitive to encounters with others, since Christ may meet the church in strangers (see Matt. 25:31–46).[24] Like faithfulness meeting the community traveling with Jesus in those who are labeled the unfaithful, we meet Christ in unlikely persons.

This sketchy discussion of the travel narrative of the Gospel of Luke helps us see ourselves as a community of faith on the way with Christ and to glimpse the surprising reversal God is working through him. The glimpses may become even clearer, however, with the journey theme of Acts before us.

The Journey Theme in the Acts of the Apostles

Introduction

The story of the formation and mission of the first church begins with a second account of Christ's ascension (Acts 1:6–11; see also Luke 24:50–53). The disciples ask the risen Christ if now he will "restore the kingdom to Israel." In effect he says, "No, and it will be a much wider kingdom than you can imagine." Specifically, he promises the group of believers the power of the Spirit and commissions them to be his witnesses "in Jerusalem, in all Judea and Samaria, and to the ends of the earth" (1:6–8). The geographical range of Christ's commissioning promises the reader that travel will be a major feature of this story.

David P. Moessner concludes his study of the Lukan travel narrative with a brief overview of the function of the travel theme in Acts. He finds six sections in Acts, each of which is structured around journey. (1) In 1:16—5:42 the community takes shape out of the Pentecost pilgrims who travel to Jerusalem from all around the Mediterranean world. (2) In 6:1—9:31 the journeys of Stephen and Philip into Samaria and Gaza are recounted along with Paul's call while he is traveling to Damascus. (3) Peter's journeys through the coastal area, trips of others to Phoenicia, Cyprus, and Antioch, Peter's movement out of Jerusalem, and Paul's and Barnabas's journey from Antioch to Jerusalem are all part of 9:32—12:25. (4) The travels of Paul and Barnabas comprise the content of 13:1—15:35. (5) Paul's so-called second journey and more are recounted in 15:36—19:20. (6) In 19:21—28:31 Paul returns to Jerusalem and is then taken to Rome.[25] The Acts story is packed with travels.

Some have seen a parallel between the gospel's travel narrative and the extended section of journey that concludes Acts, 19:21—28:31.[26] Whether or not such a parallel structure is important, in the second volume readers of Luke-Acts confront another and much longer adventuresome journey with its own surprises.

Surprises on the Way

The earliest church was caught off guard by what it learned about God's propensity for reversals. The discussion that follows makes no pretense to treat the whole of the travels in Acts. It will be enough for us to sample three of the same surprising reversals in the story of the earliest church that we found in the gospel's travel narrative.

The Powerless Are Powerful. The first surprise for the earliest Christians is the fulfillment of Jesus' promise of the Spirit. The concept of the Holy Spirit is rich in both the Lukan writings, but above all this author makes it clear that God's Spirit empowers the church. At both the end of the gospel (Luke 24:49) and the beginnings of Acts (1:8), the risen Christ promises his followers "power" (*dynamis*). The gift of the Spirit is associated with power (Acts 10:38) and is frequently used to characterize the church and its witness (e.g., 4:8, 33 and 6:8). It is the church's power that most often excites questions, controversy, or awe (e.g., 3:12; 4:7; and 8:19). Most frequently evidence of the Spirit's presence marks new believers (e.g., 2:38; 4:31; 8:14–17; 9:17; 15:7–9; and 19:1–7). God certainly does more for the church through the Spirit than empower it (e.g., guidance—8:29 and 13:2), but for Luke the Spirit's presence results in enablement.

The Pentecost story in 2:1–42 exemplifies the power that comes with the Spirit. After Jesus' departure, his band of followers remain together and take care of business (1:12–26). But without their leader they are at best an embryonic community unsure of its purpose and future. The dramatic story of the outpouring of the Spirit changes all that. Luke suggests that the Spirit enables communication among the Jews gathered in Jerusalem from all over the Greco-Roman world. Equally important is that in the wake of the "tongues of fire" Peter makes the church's first public witness (2:14–40) and with remarkable results (2:41–42). We are surprised too that this empowering gift is similar to Jesus' own experience in his baptism (Luke 3:21–22). Like their Lord, the disciples are filled with the Holy Spirit (e.g., Luke 4:1 and 18). An otherwise powerless little band of believers finds new strength and courage for its mission through the Spirit. The power Jesus had given to some (Luke 9:1–6 and 10:1–20) now showers down on the whole church.

The Needy Are Blessed. Through the power of the Spirit's presence the earliest church acted in ways that Acts calls "signs" (e.g., 4:16). The expression "signs and wonders"—or variations on it—is sprinkled through the first half of Luke's story (Acts 2:22, 43; 4:30; 5:12; 6:8; 7:36; 8:13; and 15:12). Among other wondrous acts, healings are sometimes called signs (e.g., 4:22).[27]

Like Jesus, the church attends to the needy through healing. For example, the story is still in its first phase when Peter and John encounter a man lame from birth. Like other such afflicted persons he is dependent on the generosity of others. They heal him, and the crowd is filled with "wonder and amazement" (3:1–10). The story is conspicuous in the way it parallels Jesus' own healings (e.g., Luke 5:17–26). Even as Jesus raised those taken to be dead (e.g., Luke 7:11–17), the earliest

Christians in Acts are empowered to do the same (e.g., Acts 9:36–42 and 20:7–12).[28]

The needy are proved blessed through the church's ministry to all kinds of human afflictions. The narrator sometimes offers summaries of such ministry (as in 5:16; 8:7; and 19:11–12). In their command over unclean spirits the first Christians demonstrate the same authorization we saw in Luke 10. In Philippi a slave owner exploits for his own profit a girl possessed by a demon; but Paul orders the demon out of her, and she is freed (Acts 16:16–18). The rather odd story in 19:13–20 suggests Jesus' own authority present in Paul and the others.

The Christian community in Acts cared for the needy within its own ranks as well as those outside the church. The narrator tells us of how in the church "no one claimed private ownership of any possessions, but everything they owned was held in common" (4:32). But with the story of Ananias and Sapphira the author is honest enough to describe how such a system broke down as a result of human sinfulness (5:1–11). When the widows of the "Hellenists" within the community were neglected, the community selected servants assigned to correct the neglect (6:1–4).[29] Luke here suggests how the community organized itself to serve those in need.

In the Acts story of the early church, the Christian community discovers and continues to enact God's radical reversal of the human condition. As integral as that reversal is to the gospel's portrait of Jesus' ministry, the turnabout of the needy is equally central to the life of the church chronicled in Acts. Trained as they were on the way with Jesus to attend to the needy, the leaders of the first church received power to transform the lives of the afflicted.

Something more may startle us about these first two surprises along the way—the powerless are powerful and the needy blessed. They each parallel Jesus' own ministry. Like its Christ, the church receives empowerment for ministry through the Spirit. Then the earliest Christians continued many of the same features of Jesus' ministry, most notably the reversal of the plight of the needy. Christ's ministry continues in the church's ministry! (Is that part of what Paul might mean by claiming the church is the body of Christ—1 Cor. 12:12–27 and Rom. 12:4–5?) The impact of that surprising turn of events still reverberates in the church today. How surprising it is that God entrusts to us a portion of Christ's ministry. When we have the courage and the trust to follow God's leading through the Spirit, we may be surprised by the church's power to alter the conditions of the needy.[30]

The Unfaithful Are Faithful. Certainly the most prominent reversal of the church's self-understanding in Acts comes with the inclusion of Gentiles in the community. Again their experience is based on what they learned on the way with Jesus, namely, that faith arises where one might least expect it. But in this case the church's journeys with the Spirit lead them even farther than the disciples had gone with Jesus.

In Luke's gospel Jesus' ministry is restricted to Galilee and Judea. The third evangelist narrates Jesus' unsuccessful effort to enter a Samaritan village (Luke 9:52–53), reports his encounters with both Samaritans and Gentiles on Jewish soil (e.g., Luke 17:11–19 and 7:1–10), and recounts his parables in which non-Jewish characters emerge as heroes (e.g., Luke 10:25–37). His ministry, however, never takes him beyond the regions of Galilee and Judea.[31] Luke reserves for the church's mission the passage of the gospel message beyond Jewish territory (Acts 1:8). For that reason the church on the way with the Spirit goes into uncharted waters. The church in Acts operates initially on the assumption that Christian faith is a form of the Jewish religion, that Christianity is a sect group within Judaism. But the unmapped way leads the church to a startling and controversial discovery: Gentiles are capable of faith.

The earliest church moves in stages toward that decisive discovery. First, Jews who live beyond the borders of Palestine are among those who witness the outpouring of the Spirit and become believers in Christ (Acts 2). Some of them are doubtless Gentiles who have converted to Judaism. Then the good news is preached in Samaria with remarkable success (8:5–8). The once despised ethnic half-breeds, whose religion is regarded as a Jewish heresy, are incorporated into the Christian community. The church discovers Jesus' declarations that Samaritans are capable of faith (Luke 17:11–19) and righteousness (Luke 10:30–37).

Philip's encounter with the Ethiopian eunuch on the road to Gaza (8:26–39) brings a still more startling discovery. Deuteronomy 23:1 explicitly excludes eunuchs from "the assembly of the Lord." Now one of the ostracized demonstrates a willingness to believe and is baptized. Furthermore, Ethiopians are regarded as a people far removed in a mysterious land.[32] Philip boldly goes beyond the sanctions of Judaism and Palestinian culture to enable faith in one thought to be incapable and unworthy of belief. The story of the eunuch's baptism anticipates the gospel's journey to the ends of the earth but hints at other matters as well. Technically, the eunuch is the first Gentile received into the church, but he is also one whose sexuality has banished him from those who might be among God's people. His baptism is a significant step in the church's mission. The next step along the way is, however, more complicated.

The Ethiopian eunuch may have been the first Gentile to be baptized, but Peter's provocative vision reported in 10:9–16 launches the church toward the discovery that Gentiles in general are capable of faith. He is at a loss to know what the vision means. A sheet filled with all kinds of unclean creatures is accompanied by a voice inviting him to kill and eat them. Like the good Jew he is, Peter refuses, but the voice persists in ordering him to eat the unclean food: "What God has made clean, you must not call profane!" (10:15). In the meantime, an angel visits Cornelius, a Caesarean centurion, asking that he summon Peter to his home (10:1–8). Cornelius's willingness to believe the Christian message clarifies Peter's vision for him. Peter summarizes his discovery in a speech in the centurion's house: "God shows no partiality" (10:34). When the Gentiles gathered in Cornelius' home receive the gift of the Spirit as a result of Peter's words, the Jewish Christians with Peter are "astounded," and the first explicitly Gentile Christians are baptized (10:44–48). The church beholds the impartiality of God's grace in Christ.

Peter reports his experience to the church in Jerusalem, but meets opposition from those who are called "the circumcision believers (party)" in Acts (11:2). Nonetheless, the fact that the Spirit was ahead of the church and moving among the Gentiles forces them to admit, "Then God has given even to the Gentiles the repentance that leads to life" (11:18).

Still the church is reluctant to change its perspective, much like the church of our time. Some go about preaching to the Gentiles (e.g., 11:19–24 and 13:44–47), but the issue is not yet settled. Others persist in the conviction that Gentiles must first become Jews before they can embrace the Christian message. That group (sometimes called "the sect of the Pharisees," e.g., 15:5) eventually comes into conflict with Paul and Barnabas (15:1–2). So the church gathers in Jerusalem to resolve this controversy. Luke reports that Paul's testimony of the Spirit's coming to the Gentiles prevails, and James issues the council's conclusion. Gentile Christians should not be burdened with the whole of the Jewish law, "but we should write to them to abstain only from things polluted by idols and from fornication and from whatever has been strangled and from blood" (15:20).

With the decision of the Jerusalem council, the church finally embraces the discovery of the faithfulness of the unfaithful. However, we should note in a sidebar to our discussion of Acts that Paul tells us it was not that easy. In Galatians 2 he seems to recount the same gathering in Jerusalem (though this is debated) and the agreement that James, Peter, and John would work among the Jews and he and Barnabas among the Gentiles. (Note, however, the one qualification to the acceptance of Gentile believers Paul cites in Gal. 2:10.) "The circumcision faction" continues to resist change, and even Peter chickens out and refuses to continue to eat with Gentile Christians (Galatians 2:1–14). Paul may be a bit more honest than Luke in portraying the church's resistance to this radical change in its mission. By doing so, he helps us to see more clearly the parallel between the early church's struggle with this issue and our own quarrels over changes in our ministry today.

The Lukan description of the discovery that Gentiles were objects of God's care and the Spirit's work involves still further surprises. Paul is reported again and again to have engaged the cultures where his travels took him. As a Jew born and raised amid Gentiles, he was better equipped than Peter and some of the other first followers to do so. What interests us is that Paul was not always successful when he entered into dialogue with those various cultures. (See 19:8 and 9 in which the Greek word *dialegomenos* is perhaps unfortunately translated "argued.") At the Areopagus in Athens the adroit Paul speaks the language of the culture, but his listeners stumble over his appeal to the resurrection of the dead. The results of his efforts are at best limited (17:16–34). The Spirit leads the church to the Gentiles, but that does not always mean the gospel message evokes a believing response among them.

The discussion has rather carefully chronicled the story of the church's revisioning of its mission to include Gentiles because the tale so clearly represents several realities of being on the way with God's Spirit. First, of course, this reformation in the church's self-understanding is arguably the most important change the Acts account reports. In effect it transformed the church from a Jewish sect into a universal movement, without which most of us would not be Christian today. Second, this story suggests that the church's life continues to move through progressive discoveries that stretch us farther even than the followers of Jesus were led. This is true of the church today. The Spirit continues to move out ahead of the church, leading it again and again into new revelations of how those we think of as unfaithful prove to be ready to believe. Herein lies the danger of some uses of the Bible to determine the church's mission. If the earliest church was not limited in its mission to what Jesus did, perhaps the contemporary church is not limited to what the Bible prescribes. Might not the Spirit lead us beyond scripture, as she led the early church beyond the borders of Jesus' ministry?[33]

Finally, and as already noted, the story of the early church's redirection toward the Gentiles demonstrates the dynamics of resistance to change. Those dynamics differ little from the ones we experience in the contemporary church. Being the church on the way with the Spirit is unnerving in the dramatic changes it entails. Martin Forward summarizes the meaning of this surprise:

> The people of God whom Luke describes were learners in God's wide world, and to read of them reminds us that as we meet people of different religions and cultures, sharing the good news with them can teach us of God as well as them.[34]

God continues to surprise us with radical reversals as we travel into the future with the Spirit.

Conclusion

In Acts the first church is surprised along the way in at least these three ways: The powerless are powerful; the needy are blessed; and the unfaithful are faithful. It goes without saying that there is much more in the Acts story than what we have gathered under these three enigmatic reversals. Still, they afford us a peek into the dynamics of the community's journey under the leadership of the Spirit.

The conclusion of the story offers its own unique shock. As Jesus had promised, the gospel is carried to the ends of the earth (i.e., Rome). Yet the one who brings it there is a prisoner in chains. The route to the destination is not what we expected.[35] In the gospel story the disciples follow Jesus to Jerusalem, but there they learn the destination was actually a cross and an empty tomb. In Acts the church follows the Spirit to the ends of the world in Paul, but little did they anticipate that the gospel would first be preached there by one arrested and imprisoned much like their Lord.

The Acts story, of course, never really ends. We are left with Paul under house arrest, awaiting his hearing with Caesar. Even there and under those conditions he "welcomed all who came to him, proclaiming the kingdom of God and teaching about the Lord Jesus Christ with all boldness and without hindrance" (28:30–31).[36] The journey is not done, even though Paul has reached the church's destination at "the ends of the earth" (1:8). The Spirit entices the church still farther, and the journey continues. So we dare not assume that the surprises of following the Spirit on the way are exhausted with the conclusion of the Acts story. The conclusion of that book hints that just the opposite is true. "The rest of the story" can be found in the ongoing saga of the church's movement through nineteen more centuries and beyond. And with the continuation of the story, the surprises continue.

One more note before concluding our survey of journey in Luke and Acts. Interestingly, the gospel narrative concludes with Jesus' command to his followers to stay put: "[S]tay here in the city until you have been clothed with power from on high" (Luke 24:49b). They will eventually be led out from Jerusalem as Jesus had led them to that city. When to travel and when to stay put? The interim between traveling with Jesus and traveling with the Spirit makes an important point. Christians travel with God present. In the gospel story God in Christ is the disciples' traveling companion. In Acts God moves with the church through the Spirit. The church is not alone on the way, and when the divine presence is absent (between Jesus' ascension and the outpouring of the Spirit) the community stays put!

We do well today to heed that provocative suggestion. The church changes as it is able to discern the Spirit ahead of it. Without such a discernment, we are liable to the whims and fancies of our own desires and stubbornness. Our divine traveling companion provides us the direction of our route. The church today is still dependent on the capacity to perceive God's presence on the road ahead. Like the early church we need one another in community to make out the elusive Spirit we follow.

When it appeared that the unfaithful Gentiles were capable of belief, the church gathered to discuss the matter. Through dialogue with one another, respectful listening to our Christian sisters and brothers, and appreciative sensitivities to others, God leads us into and through change after change.

Conclusions

Unifying the Image

The goal of the conclusion of the study of Luke-Acts and the journey theme found there is to unify and assess the image "on the way" in terms of its promise for the church today. The passages in Luke-Acts provide raw material out of which emerges a single metaphor for the church's self-understanding today. The substance of this biblical material suggests what Robert Brawley in his study of the narrative world of Luke-Acts has called "Progressive Discovery."[37] The discussion has attempted to flesh out the content of that discovery in terms of the surprises the followers of Jesus encountered on the way to Jerusalem and the first church experienced on the way to "the ends of the earth" with God's Spirit.

Those surprises entailed God's radical reversals of the common cultural understandings the bodies of believers brought to their travels. In order to capture something of the element of astonishment each entailed, the investigation has attempted to express these inversions with statements that have a little of the character of metaphorical shock and disruption.

1. *The Unfaithful Are Faithful.* Believers always construct stereotypes of those who are capable of faith and those who are not. The Jews, including Jesus' followers and even Jesus himself, came with such boundaries in place between the righteous and the unrighteous. But, following Jesus' own discovery, the disciples saw those borders violated again and again as they progressed toward Jerusalem. The church presupposed such borders in its own mission even as it was given them by the risen Christ. But the Holy Spirit traveled ahead of them and lured them into new visions of their mission.

2. *The Needy Are Blessed.* The needy, it seems, must be deprived of God's blessing. Their condition is inextricably welded to human sinfulness, be it their own or their ancestors. In Christ, God turns such an understanding on its head and shows a special concern for the afflicted, injured, and disabled (either physically or emotionally, that is, by demonic possession). His followers heard Jesus say this and practice it in his associations and in his healings and exorcisms. The church found itself empowered to continue Jesus' own ministry to the needy.

3. *The Highest Place Is the Lowest.* As God was upsetting the condition of the needy, so too was the divine work in Christ turning upside down the cultural conceptions of greatness. Jesus not only taught such a reversal of values but in his own death as an innocent victim demonstrated it for the sake of humanity. Disciples are shocked by such an inversion and resist internalizing it. It is a surprise not easily conceived, much less practiced.

4. *The Powerless Are Powerful.* Along with our conceptions of greatness, our assumptions about power get undermined on the way with Jesus and the Spirit. We assume the powerful are those in high positions who hold the destiny and well-being of others in their decisions. That makes most of us imagine ourselves defenseless against the forces of human power and even more of cosmic, transcendent power. Jesus empowers his followers for mission with authority that astonishes us, and then God does the same for the church with the gift of the divine Spirit. Power must entail something more than earthly or transcendent station. How else would followers of Jesus and the Spirit command even the unclean spirits of our world and our culture?

Something like these enigmatic surprises comprise the "Progressive Discovery" of being on the way with Jesus and the Spirit. What might the progressive discoveries of the church be in its present season of change, if we were to image ourselves on a journey with God? A good metaphor is filled with paradoxical qualities. Does the image "on the way" hold within itself sufficient contradictions to be intriguing and tantalizing?

If the church should image itself as a community of faith on the way, several tensions result. The first is tension between being fixed, positioned, and established in the world as Christ's witnesses, while at the same time traveling into the future led by the Spirit. If we are on the way, we know who we are but, at the same time, are surprised by who we are to become. The church represented to us in the Acts narrative knew they were Christ's witnesses to the whole world but had no idea that they would become a universal church breaking out of the boundaries of its parent faith—Judaism.

The second tension is implicit in the first. Being on the way entails surprises. The church is both grounded in its past and discovering its future. The first church had no doubt about its roots in Christ's ministry, death, and resurrection but still had to learn its full identity in the experience of the Holy Spirit. Each of the surprises we found in the Luke-Acts material contains an "is" and an "is not." The unfaithful are the faithful, but also remain the unfaithful. The highest place is the lowest, so how is it "high"? In a sense the church is and is not "on the way," for while being in process of becoming we are still the body of Christ, the community of faith, the people of God.

Insofar as these paradoxical tensions are conscious, the image of the church as the community of faith on the way is provocative and ceaselessly intriguing. To put it another way, we are in progressive discovery, even while in faith we hold firm to God's declaration of our nature and mission.

The Merits of the Image

The dynamics of the image of "on the way" suggest that change is an integral part of the church's being in the world. The church cannot refuse to change, since it is in process of discovery. Under the influence of the dynamics of this image, the church cannot change willy-nilly with the currents of culture, because it knows it follows God's Spirit. But for the same reason neither can it resist all change. We are left with an openness to change, a willingness always to weigh the possibility that change is one of the progressive discoveries of our life as a church.

But does the reframing of the classic image of Christian journey or pilgrimage with that of being on the way make any difference? The study of journey in Luke and Acts demonstrates that it does.

First, the Lukan material makes it clear that the church's travel is always and fundamentally communal and not individualistic. Jesus' followers formed a community in which relationships with the total group were more important than the individuals that comprised it. The church in Acts follows the Spirit as an assembly of Christians. Even Paul is no lone ranger, as a careful reading of Acts shows. See, for instance, the constant presence of a colleague (e.g., Barnabas) and the use of the inexplicable "we" in the Acts story (16:10–17; 20:5–15; 21:1–18; and 27:1—28:16).[38] Moreover, we know from his letters that Paul constantly worked with companions in his ministry (e.g., 1 Cor. 1:1).

Second, in contrast to some expressions of the classic journey image, with the image of the church on the way the destination is known in one sense but in another sense remains unknown. In the travel section of the Gospel of Luke, the disciples may know the destination is Jerusalem, but they do not understand that the cross is the actual destination in that city. In Acts the destination is announced in 1:8 as "the ends of the world." Still, the church does not know either how that destination is reached (Paul in chains) or its destination as a universal faith beyond the borders of Judaism. Even if the destination is in some sense known, the route is discovered along the way.

Third, the classic imagery of Christian journey has sometimes implicitly sanctioned disengagement from culture. The biblical materials we have studied in the construction of the image of way accentuate an engagement with culture (e.g., Paul's dialogue with various cultures in

Acts) and deep attachment to others, especially those in need. In this manner, the way image tends to emphasize and facilitate relationships and social responsibility. Moreover, it is fundamentally world-affirming, consistent with the biblical theme of the goodness of creation.[39] The way is above all a path of service and mission.

Fourth, Crabtree proposes two criteria for assessing the value of any image: (1) That any image needs to be truthful and held in relationship with others and (2) that it be useful. The truthfulness of the image on the way is found in its tension with both the images of the church as "homing" (chapter 4) and "stumbling in the light" (chapter 5). The tension created among these in the formula "the church is a community of faith on the way home stumbling in the light" guards the phrase "on the way" from becoming an all-sufficient self-understanding for the church. The usefulness of the image "on the way" is promising for a number of reasons. It is related to the classic and familiar image of journey and therefore is not entirely foreign. It is solidly biblical both in its prominence in Luke-Acts and elsewhere in scripture. Furthermore, it resonates with the church's current experience of rediscovering itself in a new cultural setting with a revised mission and missional strategy.

Finally, the elucidation of being on the way underscores that God is the church's traveling companion. Insofar as Luke-Acts suggests that the community of the disciples and church are not to travel without the divine presence, the image implies that God is on the way with the church. Jesus is the model for the disciples' detection of how faith arises in unlikely persons. That hints that Christ himself participated in surprising discoveries. The further implication is that the pilgrim God participates in the church's discoveries.

"On the way" therefore holds promise for enabling the church today to imagine its life in the process of change, something that the traditional journey metaphor has not always succeeded in doing. But being on the way implies direction, destination, and goal. How does the New Testament speak of the point to which the way leads us? We next turn to that question.

CHAPTER FOUR

"Homing"

"The church is a community of faith on the way home."

The prophet Ezekiel is directed to speak these poetic words: "But you, O mountains of Israel, shall shoot out your branches, and yield your fruit to my people Israel; for they shall soon come home" (Ezek. 36:8). Most likely these words were addressed to Israel in exile. Through the prophet God promises the exiles a homecoming. Their homeland was originally God's gift, and now after their time dispersed in foreign lands they will again be led back home. That image of God bringing the people home imprinted itself on the consciousness of Israel, and the first Christians inherited that imprint. Home is a profoundly traditional religious symbol for both Jews and Christians.

"Homing" is the second of the metaphors in the New Testament that comprise the broader one that I propose we might reclaim for the church in a new era. From a number of New Testament passages, this chapter endeavors to fashion the process of seeking a home and home-making itself into a metaphor that represents Christian discipleship in our contemporary culture. Before beginning the investigation of New Testament passages, however, it is necessary to consider the reasons for selecting homing as a central metaphor for the church's identity.

Metaphorical Promise

"Homing" is promising as a central image of the church for several reasons. It is both an ancient and fundamental metaphor and one that is alive in our own culture. "Home" has been called one of the fundamental metaphors that has spawned a range of other metaphorical expressions. Paul Ricoeur says "the metaphor of the home is really 'a metaphor for metaphor…'"[1] In his provocative study of 1 Peter (which we will examine below), John H. Elliott summarizes the "compelling force" of home "as a symbol of communal identity and basis of ethos." His summary cites four reasons for its power, which may be paraphrased this way: Home and family are universal experiences. Their language is inherently versatile so that they can be used in different contexts and with a variety of references. They reflect the practical realities "of everyday economic and social necessity (the business of maintaining a home and a place of livelihood)." Finally, at an emotional level they embody our common experience of seeking a home, achieving a place of belonging, and knowing companionship. Furthermore, Elliott writes, "As *oikos* [home] symbolizes the bonds which unite, it also implies the factors which divide."[2] Consequently, home and homing carry within themselves an ambivalence rooted in emotional memory and sometimes current experience.

Home and homing in fact today comprise a common image for speaking of a destination, a place of rest, and a base for living. In our culture home is often used as a kind of symbol for the ideal. It expresses a goal we seek to achieve. "To make a house a home" (homemaking) is a process many today clearly understand, even if they do not always articulate their dream with precisely that expression. Many also know the ambivalence of home. Home may represent more division than unity, turmoil rather than peace, and violence instead of love. For those whose experience of home is negative, an ideal home has that much more appeal. In other words, home-homing is a living metaphor, one that resonates with our contemporary experience and is rich with appeal and meaning. So rich is it that we may not know all that we mean by home. If we should ask another what they mean by home—after having said the obvious (e.g., "a place where I live" or "where I was raised")—she or he would have trouble expressing what it means. So a basic symbol deeply embedded in human consciousness is very much alive in our own day but equally provocative and sometimes puzzling.[3]

This chapter exploits the promise of the metaphor of homing in terms of its quest, that is, of going home, finding a home, or making a home. Religiously the larger metaphorical realm of home implies a process or a journey. Consequently, it is closely linked with the metaphor of the way explored in chapter 3. In the simplest sense, homing imagines a search for or a passage to a divinely given destination. We are not at home, and we seek to identify a destination we can call home and arrive at that condition. Home is a future destination for us, and going home is the process by which we hope we arrive at a new future. At the same time, home conjures the past and our origins. As a Christian image homing integrates our sense of the past, our present longings, and our anticipation of the future.

Finally, homing comprises the second proposed image for the church's self-understanding because it is deeply rooted in the language of the New Testament, indeed in the whole of scripture. Elliott observes, "Throughout the various stages of Old Testament social history the household also served as a basis of communal self-definitions of the people of God."[4] This does not mean that we can claim only those passages in which the word "home" appears, though some of those will be used in structuring the image. More important to this inquiry is the fact that home and seeking home are implicit in other New Testament language. These images are concealed within other images. The translation of the biblical themes into the image of homing entails detecting that image in scripture from our own cultural perspective.

This chapter initially treats three minor contributions to homing and related metaphors for Christian life. Then it examines three New Testament books (1 Peter and Hebrews) or portions of books (the Gospel of John) where the theme is more important. A conclusion tries to pull the common threads in all these passages into an unified image and make some observations about the relative promise and potency of the image for the contemporary church.

Bifocal Perspectives

Actually there are few New Testament passages in which home or homing is explicitly used to speak of Christian life and hope. Instead, we find a number of associated images, each of which functions in the way home and homing has been described. These three contributions will provide a first and general glimpse into an early Christian self-understanding.

Ephesians—Grow Up!

We begin with Ephesians, where in chapter 2 the author (whether it be Paul or one of his disciples) speaks of Christians as those who once were "dead" but through God's love in Christ have been made "alive" (2:1–6). Gentile Christians were once "aliens" and "strangers" to the community with whom God had made covenant. The author claims, however, that now in Christ they are "brought near" and made "citizens with the saints and also members of the household of God (*oikeioi tou theou*)" (2:11–19). They have been brought home to the Christian community. The imagery then changes to that of the community as a building that "grows into a holy temple in the Lord." Christians are structured "into a dwelling place for God" (2:20–22). This eclectic mixture of verbal pictures exposes the way in which Gentiles have been incorporated into a new community that will constitute God's home in the world.

Gentile Christians have been brought to a new home which is still in the process of "growing up" into a temple (the making of a new home).

Elsewhere this epistle further stresses the process of a maturation that is part of being in Christian community. It speaks in 4:11–16 of the "building up (*oikodomen*) of the body of Christ" until all come "to maturity, to the measure of the full stature of Christ." The household of which we are part is where we "grow up…into Christ." Growth, therefore, seems to be an essential dimension of the Christian community.

Ephesians also makes explicit the tension between what God has already done in the community and what is as yet just promised. The body of believers is already the location of God's presence in the world, but at the same time that community looks to the future for its full maturation. (See, for instance, the references to "hope" in 1:18 and 4:4.) That same tension is evident in that the author can claim Christians have already been raised from the dead (2:4–6) and immediately go on to speak of what God will do "in the ages to come" (2:7). In the view of many, Ephesians suggests the church is where God has already fulfilled the promises for the end of the age.[5]

The homing image is enriched by Ephesians in at least these ways: The church constitutes a home for Christians, but it is a home in the process of maturation. While the emphasis is on what God has already accomplished in Christ for the formation of the church, Ephesians still uses language that points beyond the present and into the future. Homing is "growing up" toward that which God has already done and is yet to do.

Pauline Fragments—Being Clothed

Like Ephesians, Paul's use of home imagery is both restricted and blended with other expressions. In a rather obscure passage in 2 Corinthians 5 Paul begins by contrasting an "earthly tent" and a "building from God." The passage is actually a continuation of the section that begins in 4:7 with the image of "clay jars." We are clothed in a temporary shelter where we suffer and yearn for clothing that will prepare us for another time. The apostle then speaks of two homes—one "in the body" (*sōmati*) separated from the Lord and one "with the Lord" (5:1–9). Paul appears to be speaking of two kinds of life, or perhaps more exactly of two periods of time. (See also Phil. 3:20.)

In Galatians 4:25–26 Paul contrasts two Jerusalems (see Revelation below). One is the earthly city that is in slavery and the other is the free "Jerusalem above." Paul seems to think of two existences as well as two cities. The one is the existence of the physical body pictured as a temporary dwelling, which nonetheless is wrapped in baptismal clothing. The other is the life of the resurrected body where believers are united with God in another age. The distinction again is between two times or ages—

one present and one yet to come. As one commentator concludes, "Believers are called to live out their lives in this age as those who ultimately, and thus in a decisive sense already, belong to another age."[6]

Elsewhere Paul employs similar language when speaking of the hope of resurrection (1 Cor. 15:35–57). There he speaks of two kinds of bodies (sōmata), the one he calls "earthly" or "physical" and the other "heavenly" or "spiritual" (1 Cor. 15:40 and 44). The first is "dust" and "perishable"; the second "heavenly" and "imperishable" (15:42 and 48). The resurrection, Paul says, involves the transformation of our modes of existence from mortal and perishable to immortal and imperishable (15:52–54). We cannot attempt an interpretation of Paul's view of the resurrection.[7] All that is necessary is to suggest that he expresses a view of human earthly life as transitional. The Christians' eventual destiny is another life in a different form in a new age.

Paul's bifocal perspective of two ages has at least three discernible elements: Our alienation in the present age from a divinely intended home ("away from the Lord" in a life of "dust"), the process of going home (being "further clothed"), and going home in the age to come to be "with the Lord" as spiritual bodies. The sharp distinction between physical life and a final dwelling with God is compromised by that process that Paul alludes to as being clothed "so that what is mortal may be swallowed up by life" (2 Cor. 5:4). The apostle further clarifies home as the condition God brings about in the future, even though it may be anticipated here and now. Home is found in another age promised by God, but that future time impacts the present insofar as it makes the future present and motivates commitment to the homing process of living the future now.

Revelation—God's Homing

Akin to the clearer imagery of Hebrews (to which we will turn shortly) is the poetic use of Jerusalem and Zion in the Apocalypse of John. Without attempting an interpretation of the elaborate imagery of this provocative writing,[8] it is enough to say that at the center of John of Patmos' work is the contrast between two homes or cities—Babylon and Jerusalem. The pictures of the first depict the evil of the world (e.g., the devastation of Babylon in chapter 18), and the images of the second portray the community of the faith resulting from God's victory over evil. In the climax of God's victory the prophet sees "the holy city, the new Jerusalem" descend from above. A voice interprets this descent with the announcement that "the home [skēnē, dwelling or tabernacle] of God is among mortals. He will dwell with them as their God; they will be his people" and suffering will be abolished once and for all (21:1–4). The city will have no temple or light because God's presence and divine glory will be immediate (21:22–23).

Viewed through the overlay of our image of homing, Revelation supplies several important features. The first is clearly the divinely initiated character of the home Christians seek and its bestowal at the end of history as we know it (i.e., eschatological). Like Paul's argument for the Christians' resurrection, Revelation stresses that God alone brings the heavenly city to Christians, and that divine gift is in the future known now only as promise. Second, John's vision plants Christians in the midst of an evil-ravaged world, an evil whose strength and perseverance the book consistently and vividly portrays.

Finally, the seer assigns great importance to faithfulness and witness as the process by which Christians participate in going home to the city God will provide. Far from being merely passive recipients of God's triumph (a frequent misreading of Revelation), Christian witness over against the incarnations of evil contributes to the divine defeat of evil. This theme is found, for instance, in the frequent expression, the one "who conquers" (e.g., 2:7, 11, 17, 26; 3:5, 12, 21; 12:11; 15:2 and 21:7). Likewise, the role of faithful witness is evident in the visions of the souls seen under the heavenly altar (6:9–11). They have given their lives in witness and are among those who have not worshiped the beast (20:4). Elisabeth Schüssler Fiorenza has persuasively argued that Revelation seeks to foster Christian resistance to a demonic imperial establishment.[9] In this case, going home is a process of faithful and consistent witness against overwhelming odds.

The perspective of Revelation is clearly futuristic. In some future event God will dwell fully at home in a new world, and the Christians' homing is dependent on God's promise to make a home with us. In this sense, the emphasis is quite different from that of Ephesians but similar to Paul's. Still, the divine homemaking entails a community of witness here and now, so that the temporary home of Christians is found in their engagement with society through faithful witness. With its bifocal vision the church is intent in looking toward a divinely promised future, even while it lives in faithful witness in a world very different from the one God will yet create.

Conclusions

What can we glean from this cursory treatment of passages related to the image of home and homing? A basic pattern is consistent among these varied and sometimes eclectic blendings of metaphorical language. With diverse imaginative words the Christian community is promised a home in relationship with one another and with God and Christ that is in one sense already experienced in this life and in another sense always an arrival now only promised for the future. With equally diverse images these passages sketch, or at least hint at, the route of the homecoming always with the suggestion of a community engaged in persistently trusting behavior. The theme of a bifocal existence in the now and the not-yet on the way to a divine destiny appears again and again, if in very different language and emphasis. In Revelation the vision of the future is sharper than the vision of the present. In Ephesians perhaps the present appears clearer than the future. Paul seems to see both with equal clarity.

These diverse ideas and verbal pictures can be brought together under the umbrella of home and homing. These portions of the New Testament evoke a sense of Christian corporate self-identity as a community in process of going to a divinely bestowed home. At the same time, believers have a home in the present with one another, gathered around Christ. While the home they seek is divinely given, they are responsible participants with God in the making of that home.

Belonging with the Unbelonging (1 Peter)

John Elliott provides a fresh but controversial reading of 1 Peter. He proposes there is a correlation between the expressions "aliens and exiles" (*paroikoi*) and "household" (*oikos* or "household of God," *oikos tou theou*), along with some related terms. That correlation, Elliott claims, supplies a clue both to the social conditions of the first readers of 1 Peter and the author's message to them in those conditions.

Aliens at Home

The recipients of the letter are addressed as "aliens and exiles" (2:11). Elliott insists that these expressions do not denote the readers' isolation from their heavenly homes. Rather they reflect that the first readers of 1 Peter have suffered actual geographical dislocation and as a result of that dislocation are estranged from the institutional systems of the region in which they live. He argues that the author addresses not the readers' spiritual state but

> that now Christians, like God's Israel of old, find themselves in an analogous situation of actual social and religious estrangement and alienation...1 Peter is a letter addressed to resident aliens and visiting strangers who, since their conversion to Christianity, still find themselves estranged from any place of belonging.[10]

Elliott's sociological analysis of 1 Peter involves the role of home or house (*oikos*) in the first century. In the Greco-Roman world, the household was the basic social unit and provided the model for all other larger structures, indeed the very essence of community itself. For Christians, too, the concept of home functioned as the focal point for their community. Consequently, the problem for the original readers of 1 Peter was their relationship with their culture, Elliott claims. The author of this letter attempts to provide its recipients with a sense of community solidarity over against their alienation from the society of the region. They are a household in themselves, the household of God. (See the metaphors used in 2:9–10 for the community's corporate identity.)

First Peter's author welds the letter's various announcements and admonitions to this central effort to cultivate a communal identity among the readers. In this sense, the letter fuses identity with responsibility. Elliott claims (to use the language of our study and not his) that "household of God" provides a root metaphor around which the author's other metaphors are clustered. The resulting message is that Christians should remain aliens in their culture.

> [I]n the Christian community all the homeless have a home in the household of God… The strategy of 1 Peter, therefore, was to motivate the communal self-consciousness and to mobilize the solidarity and steadfastness of the audience by appealing to them as uniquely graced and honored members of the household of God.[11]

Elliott's reading of 1 Peter tends to overly simplify the metaphorical language of the text. The criterion for discerning when an expression is used to refer to the first readers' "spiritual" location and when to their actual social location is at best precarious. It is possible that the terms Elliott insists are strictly social may in fact have had both a social and a religious reference. That is, Christians may have interpreted their real social alienation in terms of a sense that their final belonging was in a future and divinely instituted home. This indeed appears to be the case in the language of many of the African American spirituals in our own history. Johannine studies have sometimes claimed that the explicitly religious language of the Fourth Gospel may also be expressions of the Christian community's perception of their social situation.[12] The religious or "spiritual" and the social are not necessarily as distinct as Elliott tends to view them.

Nonetheless, Elliott's reading of 1 Peter gives us a perspective from which to understand the letter and recognize its contributions to the fashioning of a larger image of homing. Whatever its weaknesses, Elliott's interpretation helps us see several things: How important the concept of home as a place of belonging was to the earliest Christians; how Christian identity isolated them from their societies; and how essential the role of fostering community identity was for them.[13]

Conclusions and a Warning

This discussion of 1 Peter occasions three conclusions and a warning. Whether or not Elliott has overdrawn the distinction, the first conclusion is that home and homing are not purely spiritual matters but entail as well the concrete relationship of the church to its culture. The second conclusion is that cultivation of communal Christian identity is essential to the homing process. Finally, the grouping of the earliest Christians provided a sense of home here and now in spite of their alienation from their culture—i.e., belonging with the unbelonging.

First Peter's strong emphasis on home and home building obviously runs the danger of sectarianism.[14] In their community of faith Christians are to be a home in themselves and need not find their belonging in their society. Such a view by itself threatens to drive a wedge between the church and its culture; it pulls the church in the direction of social isolation, cultivates an attitude of arrogance, and renders it irrelevant to its culture.[15] While 1 Peter contributes significantly to a metaphor for the contemporary church's self-understanding, it also exemplifies an ever-present danger for the community of faith. How do we maintain the tension between belonging among those who do not belong to their culture, on the one hand, and still recognize our own roots and mission in a particular culture?

Wandering with a Promise (Hebrews)

The writing commonly called Hebrews provides a related but vastly different view important for the home and homing imagery. In one sense it further develops the theme of the church's separation from its culture, but does so with a fuller recognition of the land in which we find ourselves and in which God has found us.

In Search of a City

The famous description of faith in Hebrews 11 exemplifies a central theme of this New Testament document. The author recites a litany of "our ancestors" who "by faith … received approval" (11:2). Within this litany the author describes characters of faith in the Hebrew scriptures (especially Abraham and Sarah) as having grasped and trusted God's promise, then died without seeing the promise fulfilled (11:13, 39). They understood themselves as "strangers and foreigners on the earth…seeking a homeland" (*patrida*) (11:13–14). Their vision was not of what they had left behind but of what they sought. "They desire a better country, that is, a heavenly one," a "city" (*polis*) that God has prepared for them (11:15–16).

Later the author warns against apostasy and assures Christian readers of what they have received through faith. They have already "come to Mount Zion and to the city of the living God, the heavenly Jerusalem …and to the assembly of the firstborn who are enrolled in heaven" (12:22–23). This suggestion that Christians have already reached their destination is, however, qualified by another passage where the destination is still in the future. "For here we have no lasting city, but we are looking for the city that is to come" (13:14). That search involves going "outside the camp" (*paramboles*) to suffer as Jesus suffered "outside the city gate" (13:12–13). The text's language suggests the paradox of the Christians' sense of having been already brought to their destination and at the same time still anticipating a home that is beyond (outside) their life in this world. This is once again the language of the paradox of realized and futuristic eschatology—the bifocal perspective of the now and the not-yet of Christian life.

A Confident Wandering

In his commentary on Hebrews, Ernst Käsemann finds the definitive motif of the writing in 3:7—4:13. There the author of Hebrews speaks of Israel's desert wanderings and the promise of "rest" that led them on. Käsemann structures his commentary around the theme of wandering. That allows him to draw certain conclusions about the book's primary emphasis. The message of the good news comes to the Christian as it did to Israel (4:2), but the message is a call. *"The Logos grants no final revelation. It calls to a way,* the goal of which it points out by way of promise, and which can only be reached in union with the Logos and its promise." That promise hastens the people of God on in their journey. Those who receive the revelation in Christ are destined to a wandering existence as part of the community of God's people. That roving life, the interpreter argues, accounts for the preponderance of verbs of motion in Hebrews (e.g., 10:22, 36; 12:1; and13:13). The promise points us to the future. *"Faith thus becomes a confident wandering."* With this general interpretative framework Käsemann goes on to explicate the other major portions of Hebrews.[16]

There is little doubt that Käsemann overworks his interpretative perspective and is prone to reduce the whole of Hebrews to one of its important themes. But still the theme he emphasizes is in the text and presents another expression of a homeless people engaged in homing. Käsemann's most important contribution is his insistence that in Hebrews the gospel message is a call to a promise that leads the church on its way toward God's destiny, that is, toward rest. Rest becomes the essence of Christians' home (e.g., 4:1–11).

Käsemann rightly stresses that the church is a wandering community of faith, but he may not give full credit to another theme of the book. The Christian community is both seeking its divinely promised rest and in the process also experiencing it within their communal relationships. In 4:3 Christians are described as those who have already entered that rest, and 4:11 admonish readers to "make every effort to enter that rest." That is to say, along with the not-yet of the promise, there is a stronger message of the fulfillment of the promise in the present than Käsemann seems willing to acknowledge.

Conclusions

This hasty treatment of Hebrews suggests several things about the emerging image of homing: First, "rest" is an important dimension of home; second, the promise of a destination is accompanied by a sense of its partial fulfillment in Christian community; and, third, that community is a wandering people yet uncertain of where, when, and how God will fulfill the promise. The general picture we gain from these portions of Hebrews portrays the Christians' sense of being aliens in the world and looking toward a new place which is their true and full community. Christians live as homeless persons who trust God's promise to bring them to a home. The images of city, homeland, country, Jerusalem-Mount Zion, and rest all visualize the Christians' home with God. The process of homing is pictured as a wandering, seeking, desiring, coming, going, entering, and looking. The portrait is comparable to the one we found in 1 Peter, with the possible exception that the role of God's promise figures more prominently in Hebrews. Christian discipleship is a wandering with a promise. It entails a process of going home led by God's promise; but embracing that promise is in itself entering our rest.

Separated Together (The Gospel of John)

The theme of home in the Gospel of John offers a very different component for a base metaphor of homing. In this gospel Christian identity derives from Christ's identity in relationship with God. At nearly every junction in the Fourth Gospel, readers find the relationship between Jesus and God extended to include believers. For instance, Christ is portrayed as an alien in this world, who has descended to live among humans for a time before once again ascending to his heavenly home with God (see, e.g., 1:14; 3:13; 6:62; and 20:17). Consequently, Christ is "not of this world" (8:23). Those who believe in Christ share this alienation from the world, for they too "do not belong to this world" (15:19). Furthermore, the relationship between God and Christ is the model for the believers' relationship with both God and Christ (e.g., 14:10; 15:4; and 17:23).[17] The relationship between God and Christ is also the prototype for the believers' relationship with one another (e.g., 17:11) and with the world (15:18).[18] In the Fourth Gospel Christian identity, both individual and corporate, is radically Christ-centered.

Home Is Where You Dwell

The implication of such a view is that the Christian community finds its home in relationship with God and Christ as well as with one another. That theme is often expressed in the fourth evangelist's use of the verb *menō*, variously translated "abide," "remain," "dwell," or "indwell."[19] Whatever else may be suggested by the wide and frequent use of this verb in the Gospel of John, it clearly suggests an intimate relationship which is sometimes expressed with the simple word "in" (e.g., 17:23; 14:10, 11, and 20). The believers' home is a relationship with God and with Christ through the active presence (or indwelling) of the Spirit (e.g., 14:17).

Such an interpretation is further suggested by the two uses of a noun, *monē*, related to the verb *menō*. In 14:2 the *New Revised Standard Version* translates the plural form of that noun "dwelling places" but in 14:23 renders the singular form "home." The first passage is often interpreted as a promise of the believers' destiny after death,[20] but the second suggests something quite different. As a result of the believers' loving Christ and keeping his word, God and Christ will "come to them and make our home [*monēn*] with them." The first passage (14:2), therefore, seems at least to promise something in addition to a future home. Gail O'Day writes of John 14:2 that

> it is critical to the interpretation of Jesus' words here that the reference to "my Father's house" not be taken as a synonym for heaven. Instead, this reference to the Father's house needs to be read first in the context of the mutual indwelling of God and Jesus, a form of "residence" that has been repeatedly stressed from the opening verses of the Gospel…It is in this relationship, as much as in any heavenly dwelling per se, that there are "many rooms."[21]

Such a reading is strengthened by the ambiguity of "come again" in verse 3. It may refer equally to Christ's coming as resurrected Lord and/or his coming in the Spirit as well as to his future advent in glory.

God and Christ have made their home within the Christian community. Consequently, the community's home is within itself. Christians find their home in relationship with other believers and with God and Christ, who reside within the company of believers.

Where's the Glory?

In different language, Jesus' prayer in chapter 17 expresses the substance of John 14:23 (God and Christ make their home with believers). The prayer shifts in verse 20 to "those who will believe in me through" the original believers' words. Verse 22 reads in part, "The glory that you [God] has given me I have given them…" If one takes "glory" (*doxa*) in its ancient Hebraic sense of the manifest presence of God, Jesus is claiming that the sense in which God has revealed divine presence in Christ's life and ministry is now present in the church. The church as the community of believers, then, is the locus of the divine presence in the world; it is the continuing incarnation of the divine Word (1:14) in the world.[22] God's home is not in some transcendent realm but among the society of believers.

The identity of the Johannine community is centered in a relationship with God and Christ in the present—an intimate relationship in which the divine home is in and among those of the community. It may be that the gospel promises a future in which the Christians' home relationship is more immediate, as 14:2 may suggest. But the tension between the now and the not-yet in the Fourth Gospel pulls strongly in the direction of the present experience of the community.[23] That is true of the theme of home as it is of other themes related to Christians' hope for the future. On other matters, especially the promise of eternal life, the fourth evangelist seems to emphasize the fulfillment of God's promise in believers' faith in this world and life (e.g., 3:36 and 5:24).[24]

The Fourth Gospel's chief contribution to a search for the ingredients of a homing image for the Christian community is in the suggestion that as a church our home in is relationships.[25] We find our home in relationships with God and Christ through the Spirit and in how those relationships with the Divine are lived out with others in community. Yet there is still a sense in which the relationship with God and Christ will be more complete in some future existence. Hence, this gospel further strengthens the now and not-yet quality of Christian homing but clearly favors the present possibilities of belonging in relationship with God and Christ. The "glory" is in the present community of faith.

Mutuality and Mission

It might seem that such an interpretation of the church's home as a relationship here and now with God in Christ devalues the church's engagement in the world. There is clearly a sectarian quality—a sense of not belonging—to the picture of the community of believers in the Gospel of John, and that quality has been emphasized in recent scholarship.[26] The gospel seems to invite Christians to dissociate from the world. For instance, the love commandment in 15:12 speaks only of loving other believers.

However, this gospel also includes a unequivocal call for the community's mission in the world. That call is found most explicitly in the risen Christ's sending of believers as he himself had been sent into the world (20:21—see also 3:16). Again, the community's mission in the world is defined by Christ and his mission in the world. Christ further prays for believers "in the world" (17:11) and specifically asks that they not be "taken out of the world" but that they be protected in their life in the world. Even though the community does not belong to the world, their mission is there (17:15–18). The process might be diagrammatically represented this way:

The Gospel of John seems, therefore, to suggest a paradoxical tension between the church and the world. The church does not find its

Readers
and Their Situation

↕

Scripture ←——————————————→ Scripture

origin in culture but lives in mission within a culture. The Fourth Gospel articulates the essential dilemma of the church's relationship with culture. The mutuality of relationships within the community separates it from the world but also empowers it for mission in the world.

Conclusions

When viewed together, the passages discussed in this chapter create a collage of images. What can we make of these disparate snapshots of the church? An answer may be found in attempting four tasks: (1) To pull together the various expressions of the Christian community's home and its process of going home; (2) to name and summarize the tensions found in the metaphors of the passages; (3) to evaluate the strengths and weakness of the image of home and homing that have emerged from these passages; and (4) to ask how this metaphor of the church supplements that of the previous chapter—"on the way."

Unifying the Image

The features of the passages comprise threads out of which we might weave a carpet of homing underlying the church today. Those threads include at least these four:

Household. The New Testament suggests that the community of Christians constitutes its participants' home. Their most fundamental sense of belonging is derived from the social intercourse among them. This view implies a complex relationship between the Christian community and its culture. The church's home is a mobile one. Christians are camping out for a time in the world as resident aliens within a culture, and the eventual destination of their homing is beyond worldly cultures.

At least two dangers lurk within such language. The first has been characterized as a sectarianism. The church is so different from its culture that it never fully acknowledges its membership in a culture. But, second, such language also conceals the danger of an otherworldliness. A transcendent destination is more explicit in some cases (e.g., Revelation, Hebrews, and 1 and 2 Corinthians) and less so in others (e.g., 1 Peter and Ephesians). If the Christian community is at home in itself, its eventual "rest" comes only in another realm. But such a view endangers the church's relationship with its society insofar as it engenders a disengagement from culture. An otherworldly sectarianism does not foster an active commitment to improving society.

A Wandering People. The promise of this thread is the transiting nature of the church amid a culture that is changing and in which there is less and less acknowledgment of its contributions to this culture. It takes seriously the mobile quality of the church as the participants' own household and accentuates the Christians' changing experience. In doing so, the same dangers of sectarianism and otherworldliness surface.

A wandering people easily become irrelevant to their culture, and a wandering evoked by the divine promise may strengthen an attitude of otherworldliness.

Relationships. The Johannine thread contributes a sense of community centered in God, Christ, and the Spirit, as well as the community's movement into the world, sent there on mission. It magnifies the theme of the community as the Christians' home by stressing the quality of the relationships that obtain within that community. The danger is once again that the image cultivates an isolation from culture. Such a danger is minimized only insofar as the missional character of the community is emphasized and held in strict tension with the relationships of life within the community itself.

Bifocal Perspective. In each of these three images we have found evidence of the perspective articulated in the first passages we examined as minor contributions. The community's home is both in another and future age while also in this age. The church looks to the future and lives faithfully in the present. Homing is the process of clinging to a promise yet to be fulfilled and finding empowerment through that promise for its life in the present. Hence, the church's identity is found in a coalescence of the future and the present. The danger inherent in such double vision is that either the present or the future may be minimized for the sake of the other.

The carpet woven from these four strands is composed of threads pulled tightly in several directions, so that its unity is found in the very strains within itself, that is, in tensions.

Tensions in the Image

In these four strands we detect a number of important tensions in the image of homing, especially as we try to discern the full fabric of the metaphor. First, those tensions include a paradoxical stance between the now and the not yet (between promise fulfilled and promise yet unfulfilled). The church is in the process of homing, with its vision divided between what now is and what is yet to be. It is already at home here and now and still not yet at home. Second, the church is imagined as a community that knows its eventual destination and one that at the same time lives (or wanders) only out of God's promise, making the destination for the time unknown.

A third tension is discerned by virtue of the community's being stretched between an isolation from the world and a mission to the world, between disengagement from and engagement with the world. The denial of the truth of either of these poles distorts the image of the church on its way home and constitutes unfaithfulness to God's calling and the church's true identity. A fourth tension (only implicit in the New Testament materials) is that the process of homing is at the same time inherently both individual and communal. For instance, the mutual indwelling of God and Christ in the believer and the believer in God and Christ found in the Gospel of John may be individual in nature (although that is far from certain). At the same time, however, it is corporate; the divine presence is in the community and the community is in God. Finally, we have witnessed the manner in which the process of homing is accomplished by both divine and human activity. Even while God is in the process of our homemaking and ultimately responsible for it, the community is called to accept its responsibility (e.g., in witness, mission, and moral behavior).

As they pertain to the shaping of an image of homing for the church, the New Testament materials in one sense act as correctives to one another. That is, those themes that stress the otherworldliness of Christians' home modify those which stress that God has already made the divine home with the community here and now. Those that seem to stress the community as the Christians' real home qualify others that insist homing entails following a promise wherever it may lead. Focusing on what already is (we are already at home) reins in what will be (we will be brought home).

When we place the materials of these texts in dialogue with one another, they provide a balanced—however paradoxical—image. When all the passages are held in tension together, the full image is rich with possibilities precisely because of its tensional or ambiguous character. This need for interchange among different texts—for allowing the texts to interact with one another—and for embracing them all without minimizing one in favor of another, suggests that the authority of scripture is found not in isolated passages; nor does it reside in a hierarchy of biblical themes in which certain ones are taken to be more truthful than others. Authority inhabits the dialogical interchange of scripture with itself as well as with the contemporary reading community.[27] Therefore, the process of reading and interpreting scripture for the church today involves two interwoven dialogues: One conversation is between scripture and the contemporary reading community. The other is among the various portions of scripture itself.

If such a view of the authority of scripture is true, it means that we can fashion metaphors for the church's corporate self-understanding only as we engage in a three-way discussion. Such a discussion entails scripture speaking with scripture and that conversation going on in relation with our contemporary situation.

Such a process may sound complex, but none other will suffice. Otherwise, we will find ourselves focused on one part of the Bible to the exclusion of all its other components. Or, we may concentrate exclusively either on scripture alone or our own situation without a biblical context. A metaphor for the church's self-understanding arises from our listening in on conversations among portions of scripture, fully aware of our contemporary situation. Then we can allow the metaphorical tensions of scripture's language to shape our identity.

The Merits of the Image

The translation of this New Testament material into the metaphor of Christians as a community on its way home is fraught with paradoxical tension, but when each of these tensions is preserved and when the biblical themes are allowed to discourse with one another, a profound image of homing arises. It is a promising one for the church today for a number of reasons. It is biblically rooted, while at the same time reverberating with the Western human experience of a restless dissatisfaction, a sense of never quite being at home. Moreover, the image of homing is inclusive of both men and women, since both are now conceived in our culture as responsible for homemaking. The image calls and depends on what God is doing without neglect of what we are called to do. Hence it has potential for embracing social justice as part of the church's ministry.

The dynamics of the image of homing suggest that change is an integral part of the church's being in the world. The church cannot refuse to change, since it is in process of discovering, moving toward, or living its home in the world. Controlled by this image of homing, the church cannot change pointlessly with the currents of culture, because it knows its home is rooted in a divine determination. But neither can the church afford to isolate itself from culture or deny cultural change. Christian discipleship is redefined in terms of the culture in which it is exercised. If, for instance, our culture comes to practice and value cloning, Christian faithfulness requires that we take a stand on such a complicated and new ethical issue. Christian witness is redefined, too, in terms of the culture in which our witness is made. Homing entails being in the world, even if home is ultimately understood to be beyond this world.

The image of homing for the community of faith in the twenty-first century embraces a paradoxical understanding of the church's identity. Necessarily, therefore, it encourages a paradoxical understanding of reality itself, as we will argue in the next chapter.

On the Way Home

What happens when we place the home-homing image in the context of "the way"? How do these two images modify one another? To speak of the church as the Christian community on the way home reinforces a number of insights into both the homing image and the picture of the church on the way. In the previous chapter we have already noted that the metaphor of the way suggests a destination. The way is a path to something or someone. Its role in both the Gospel of Luke and the

Acts of the Apostles is to picture Jesus' disciples and the church moving toward new geographical locations. The destination is known, even if the path to that destination is filled with surprise.

If home is understood as the final destination of the Christian way, the "location" of the direction of the way becomes paradoxical. It is known and unknown; it is still in the future while present among the journeyers; it is divinely given while entailing mission along the way. The city of God prepared for the church is present in the relationships of the community with God, Christ, and one another in the midst of the journey. All the enigmatic character of being on the way with Christ and the Spirit is summarized in the ambivalent quality of the destination.

So, the church lives in its home even while seeking it. Christian life together stretches between the community of the now and the one yet to come. At one point Paul tries to capture this ambivalence with a different kind of metaphor. In his second epistle to the Corinthians, Paul twice speaks of the Spirit as God's "guarantee" to Christians (2 Cor. 1:22 and 5:5). (The *New Revised Standard Version* translates the Greek word *arrabōn* "guarantee" at 5:5 but "installment" in 1:22; see also Eph. 1:14.) In the midst of his discussion of our lives now in "earthly tents" and our lives in the new age in a "building from God," he says God "has prepared us for this very thing" by giving us "the Spirit as a guarantee" (5:5). The image is that of a "down payment" or "earnest money" on what is yet to be. Paul's image conveys something of the dilemma of the church on its way home. The divine promise of the future age is what equips and empowers the church for its life on the way. The powerless are empowered by God's first installment on the promise (i.e., the Spirit), as we saw in chapter 3. Through the Spirit the future is known and experienced at least in part in the present.

Some congregations celebrate what is called "homecoming Sunday." It is often an occasion when former members of a congregation return to worship in what was their "home church." Actually, the image of a congregation's homecoming is a very important one. In one sense, it celebrates the community in which we were first nurtured in the Christian life. In another and more profound sense, the larger body of believers is Christians' home, and a homecoming occurs each time a community gathers itself. The church is at home, even while we hope for God's future for us. Homecoming Sunday celebrates our past home, fosters the present community as our home, and still points toward another home in the future. Again, we find ourselves stretched three ways: pulled down into the present and stretched both back into the past and forward into the future.

The task of the contemporary church is to discover both the home it already is and the home it seeks on the way with God. On the way home characterizes an ambivalence the church of the twenty-first century needs to feel. With that kind of ambivalence, the reality of change can be understood and embraced as part of the process of homing. Change is integral to going home as journey is integral to the destination. Sometimes it is even said that the journey itself, and not the arrival at the destination, is the real satisfaction of travel. Might we not cultivate both satisfactions at the same time—the camaraderie of the journey on the way and the anticipation of the destination?

But to say that the church is a community on its way home requires further explorations. There is still more to say about the church's passage toward its destination. Other strata of New Testament literature illumine the identity of the church in this world, and we must now turn to that further theme to complete our metaphor. In a sense we are stumbling in the light on the way home.

CHAPTER FIVE

"Stumbling in the Light"

"The church is a community of faith on the way home
stumbling in the light."

The church stumbles in the light![1] That is perhaps the most shocking and troublesome component of the metaphorical sentence of this
study. We may be comfortable with the suggestion that the church is
"on the way." That the church seeks its divinely intended destination
(home) may not disturb us. But to say that the way of the church entails
"stumbling in the light" seems less congenial. Yet there is a clear witness
in the New Testament that such an expression has an element of truth to
it. This chapter attempts to investigate some of the New Testament passages that support this provocative phrase.

Knowing and Not Knowing

As Christians we know and yet don't know. We live within a tension between the confidence of faith and the uncertainties of belief. An
easy example is our confidence that God is involved in the world and
the events of time but our persistent uncertainty about why there is evil
and suffering in our world. If God is both good and all powerful, why
does evil exist, much less ravage our world the way it does? The Holocaust remains an insurmountable problem for Christians and Jews alike.
How could God remain silently absent amid such an atrocity as the
slaughter of millions of innocent persons?[2]

Christians cling to their faith while seeking light on such issues as
suffering and evil. As a community, we know the meaning of Anselm's

famous words, "faith seeking understanding."[3] Our lives are composed both of a fundamental belief system and a quest to comprehend our faith within a historic setting. This intrinsic and classical tension between knowing and not knowing raises perplexing questions for a church in the midst of change. How do we appropriately limit what we are confident of for the sake of what we do not know with any certainty? How does the paradox of knowing and not knowing shape our life as a community and its stance in our culture?

The church confronts these questions in a time such as ours. Tenacious forces are at work to make us change what has been the church's traditional stance in the modern world (see chapter 1). But we resist such changes because we want to preserve the integrity of our faith. Still, we may not know how our faith should respond to other changes in our culture. This may be most evident today in the moral issues surfaced in the closing decades of the twentieth century. Our faith forces us, for instance, to seek a new understanding of abortion, genetic engineering, cloning, and homosexuality. How does faith find understanding for these issues? We grope for clarity.

However, to speak of the church's search for understanding as "stumbling in the light" seems to diminish the faith out of which we search. The absence of light implies ignorance and blind groping. The New Testament use of the ancient symbols of light and darkness is, however, far more ambiguous than that. On the one hand, "to walk in darkness" implied pointless and unenlightened life. The author of 1 John contrasts walking "in darkness" and "in the light." The former is equated with sin (1 John 1:5–7). On the other hand, this same document implies Christians should acknowledge their lack of enlightenment. Having distinguished light and darkness and claimed that Christ "cleanses us from all sin," 1 John 1:8 asserts Christians do sin and to say otherwise is self-deceit and makes God a liar. Believers confess their sin and trust God's forgiveness (1:9–10). Yet elsewhere this same author declares those born of God do not sin (3:8–9; 5:18).[4]

What are we to make of this strange contradiction? Are we left in darkness or in the light? The view of light and darkness in the Gospel of John helps us understand the ambiguity of Christian life of which 1 John speaks. The prologue of that gospel calls the Word (i.e., Christ) "the light" (John 1:4) and declares "the light shines in the darkness, and the darkness did not overcome (*katalambanō*, to master) it" (1:5). In the Johannine writings "darkness" represents the world's alienation from God. John 1:5 declares the light of Christ does not annihilate sin and evil. They continue even while Christ's light shines within the world.[5] The author of 1 John captures something of the same tone in saying "the darkness is passing away and the true light is already shining" (1 John 2:8). Christians remain in the world's darkness even while they perceive and walk toward Christ's light. We stumble in the light.

The ambiguity of the church's life in a "dimmed light" is an example of biblical realism. God shows us an enlightened way, but faith continues within an ambiguous environment. The New Testament writers are sometimes brutally honest about the church's condition in the world. Jesus' disciples are portrayed as uncomprehending and even disloyal (e.g., Mark 9:32; 14:50; 66–72); they misunderstand Jesus and plead for greater clarity (John 4:31–33 and 16:29–30). In the earliest church some stubbornly resist the Spirit's guidance (e.g., Acts 15:1–2), and others are out and out disobedient (e.g., Acts 4:32, 5:1–6). In 1 Corinthians Paul addresses a series of issues in the church at Corinth, many of which exhibit its bondage to the world's arrogance and divisiveness (1:10–17 and 8:1–13). These are the same readers he says are "sanctified" (1:2); that is, they are "saints."

All of this suggests the New Testament's affirmation of the ambiguity of Christian existence as both saint and sinner. Those of us embraced by the gospel struggle to live out our faith in the world, searching for understanding and groping for faithful behavior. The church is a community of *faith, stumbling* in the light it has been granted. Such a paradoxical image captures something of the church's real experience, both in its beginnings and in the twenty-first century.

The previous chapters have already suggested how the church is engaged in a quest for understanding. Surprises "on the way" disturb and call us into question. The process of living toward "home" is no less educational. How do we discern our destination ahead of us and among us? This chapter explores two New Testament themes, each of which has to do with the church's role as a community of seekers. The first focuses on Jesus' provocative proclamation of the kingdom of God. The second theme examines the metaphorical quality of Paul's theological thought and how it implies the apostle's own effort to search for understanding of his faith.

"The Kingdom of God Is Like…"

Scholars have long thought that the focus of Jesus' preaching and teaching, at least in the first three of the gospels, is the "kingdom of God" (or "kingdom of heaven" in Matthew). That thesis has seldom been challenged in terms of its accuracy in representing the actual historical Jesus and his teachings.[6] The interpretation of the phrase "the kingdom of God" is much more complicated.

What Is the Kingdom of God?

The expression "kingdom of God" is a bit misleading in the sense that "kingdom" (*basileia*) denotes a rule or reign rather than the region over which the rule obtains. Matthew's persistent use of "kingdom of heaven" (except in four cases—Matt. 12:28; 19:24; 21:31, 43) has aided and abetted popular misunderstanding of the English translation of the phrase. That is, the kingdom of God or heaven is mistakenly equated with a place. Students of the Gospel of Matthew, however, point out that the first evangelist practices a pious Jewish avoidance of the name of God and that "heaven" is little more than a circumlocution for the word God.[7] That being the case, the phrase on the lips of Jesus refers to the presence and exertion of the divine will in a world dominated by other rules alien to God's desire.

The issue of defining what Jesus and the synoptic evangelists (Matthew, Mark, and Luke) mean by the phrase kingdom of God/heaven is still more complicated. The expression is loaded with ancient implications rooted in the Hebraic metaphor, God is king (e.g., Pss. 95:3; 97:1; 99:1). That metaphor generated the image of God's reign or dominion over the people (e.g., Ps. 2:4–9). But the divine rule was frustrated by the people's disobedience and unruliness. The prophets then spoke of God's victoriously reclaiming the rule in the world through an event known as "the day of the Lord" (e.g., Amos 5:18–24). In that day, God will restore justice in the world. But Israel's yearning for the time of divine justice went unfulfilled, and the people more and more anticipated the restoration of God's rule in the world at the "last day" as part of the final victory of the divine will. In some Jewish circles, the kingdom of God was "apocalyptic," meaning it was associated with God's grand reconstruction of creation at the end of human history (e.g., Dan. 7—12).[8]

Norman Perrin proposed that by Jesus' time the Hebraic tradition gave rise to the symbolic quality of the expression kingdom of God. By symbol he meant language that stood for larger sets of meaning. But the kingdom is a "tensive symbol" whose "meaning could never be exhausted, nor adequately expressed, by any one referent." Perrin urged us to approach the study of the kingdom in the ministry of Jesus with several things in mind:

> In the first place, "Kingdom of God" is a symbol with deep roots in the Jewish consciousness of themselves as the people of God. Then, secondly,…by the time of Jesus it had come to represent particularly the expectation of a final eschatological act of God on behalf of his people…(On the lips of Jesus) "Kingdom of God" is not an *idea* or a *concept*, it is a *symbol*. As a symbol it can *represent* or *evoke* a whole range or series of conceptions or ideas.[9]

Jesus' proclamation of the coming of the kingdom of God provoked all of Israel's dreams and longings for the future. The deepest and most fundamental human aspirations were packaged in that phrase. It was so rich that it could stimulate infinite associations and meanings. With the kingdom's advent God would right all that is wrong with us and our world. Jesus' use of the symbol touched the human desire for a better future and the fulfillment of God's every promise.[10] The establishment of God's reign, as Jesus spoke of it, was therefore an ancient symbol filled with tradition and anticipation.

The Ambiguities of the Kingdom

As a tensive symbol, the kingdom of God was in Jesus' time filled with ambiguity and intrigue. Jesus' teachings about the kingdom accentuate that tensive quality in that they are sumptuously suggestive. Most of us become confused in the process of trying to nail down exactly what Jesus taught about the coming of God's rule. Those ambiguities are important, and they ought not be swept under the rug for the sake of our need for a pretty package of thought. These are but a few of the ambiguous features of the synoptics' teachings about the kingdom:

Now or Then? On one occasion some Pharisees ask Jesus "when the kingdom of God was coming" (Luke 17:20). Their question is a good one, because Jesus' words are not consistent on the issue of when God's new reign was going to appear. At times Jesus speaks of the kingdom as future, at other times as "near," and at still others already present.

The kingdom's coming is a *future event* for which we are invited to pray (Matt. 6:10; Luke 11:2). The synoptics report Jesus' speaking in the future tense of the advent of the kingdom on several occasions (e.g., Matt. 8:11–12), not least of all with the disciples as they ate their last Passover meal with him (Mark 14:25; Matt. 26:29; Luke 22:16 18). When some supposed that the kingdom was going to appear immediately, Jesus told them the parable of the pounds (Luke 19:11–12; see also Luke 21:7–9). The words concerning those who will enter the kingdom may also imply that it is a future event (e.g., Mark 10:24; Luke 18:24; Matt. 19:24). Even when the disciples thought the risen Christ would restore God's rule in the world, Jesus assured them the timing of the kingdom was not theirs to know (Acts 1:6).

The language attributed to Jesus certainly contributes also to the impression that God's new reign is *near*. Mark's gospel begins with a summary of Jesus' message: "The kingdom of God has come near" (Mark 1:14; see also Matt. 4:17 and 10:7). All the Synoptic Gospels contain a nearly identical saying in which Jesus claims that some who are hearing him speak will "see that the kingdom of God has come with power" (Mark 9:1; Luke 9:27; Matt. 16:28). Mark 13:30 and its parallels in Matthew 24:34 and Luke 21:32 suggest the same view.

In spite of this evidence for a future or near-future appearance of God's dominion, several passages have Jesus speak as if the kingdom is already *present*. In the most striking of these, Jesus claims that if he casts out demons, then surely "the kingdom has come to you" (Luke 11:20//

Matt. 12:28). In other words, God's new rule is already at work in Jesus' authority over the forces of evil. Another equally provocative statement is found in Luke 17:21 (for which there is no parallel in either Mark or Matthew): "The kingdom of God is among you." The word translated "among" (*entos*) is ambiguous, for it can mean either "among" or "within."[11] In either case, however, the passage affirms the immediate presence of God's rule.

Scholars have vigorously debated this ambiguity concerning when the kingdom comes. G. B. Caird summarizes the three most prominent interpretations of the synoptics' representation of the timing of the kingdom's appearance. The first has been labeled "thoroughgoing eschatology." It assumes that the preponderance of the evidence favors a view that the kingdom is yet to come in the future. A second view, "realized eschatology," claims Jesus announced that the kingdom was already present in his ministry. Finally some scholars have settled on an "inaugurated eschatology." Jesus began a process by which God's renewed dominion in the world was begun, and that process continues in God's work in the present. Caird argues, however, that the ambiguity of the timing of the kingdom's fulfillment is typical of what he calls "the three tenses of salvation" in the New Testament. Like the coming of God's exercise of the divine will in the world, salvation itself is sometimes "an accomplished fact, an experience continuing in the present, and a consummation still to come." Caird in effect says that the New Testament as a whole shares this ambiguity concerning God's saving work in the world.[12]

This brief summary of the issue of the "when" of the kingdom epitomizes the equivocal character of Jesus' teachings. The bifocal tension between the now and the not-yet throughout the New Testament (see chapter 4) perhaps originates in the concept of the presence of God's rule in our world. The church can only remain suspended between the poles of the now and the then. We can only seek understanding on the boundary between God's rule as it is known in the present and anticipated in the future. The kingdom of God is like walking in the confusion of a world still not ruled by God but enlightened by glimmers of the presence of divine will at work now. Much the same is true of God's reign in another sense.

Revealed or Hidden? The evidence of the presence of the kingdom has already established that God's rule is apparent in Jesus' ministry. His authority over the demons makes that clear (Luke 11:20 and Matt. 12:28), and his resurrection declares God's immediate presence and work. Other portions of the synoptic narrative reinforce the transparent presence of God's new will for the world. One such is Jesus' free and radical reinterpretation of the Old Testament law and its interpretation in the

Judaism of his time. He forgives sin, thereby claiming for himself what was believed to be exclusively God's prerogative (e.g., Mark 2:1–12// Matt. 9:1–8//Luke 5:17–26). Moreover, he redefines regulations regarding the Sabbath (e.g., Mark 2:23–28//Matt. 12:1–8//Luke 6:1–5), fasting (e.g., Mark 2:18–22//Matt. 9:14–17//Luke 5:33–39), and divorce (Mark 10:2–12//Matt. 19:3–12; and Matt. 5:31–32//Luke 16:18). As evidence of his fulfillment of the law and the prophets (Matt. 5:17–20), the Gospel of Matthew reports that Jesus revised the law and/or its interpretation in a series of antitheses. The antithesis is between what had been taught and what Jesus now teaches: "You have heard that it was said to those of ancient time…but I say to you…" (Matt. 5:21–48). Jesus reveals God's reestablishing of the divine will for humans.

The Synoptic Gospels, however, confuse us with their talk of the "secret" (*mysterion*, "mystery") of the kingdom. In Mark, Jesus tells the story of the sower and his seeds. His disciples then ask him about the parable. In his response Jesus claims they have been given "the secret of the kingdom of God, but for those outside, everything comes in parables…" Consequently outsiders think they understand but actually do not (Mark 4:10–12; see comparable sayings in Matt. 13:11–14 and Luke 8:10). The confusing words are set within the context of Jesus' use of parables but have to do with the understanding and perception of the kingdom in Jesus' ministry. It appears there is some secret knowledge or gift needed to discern God's new reign in Jesus.[13]

The discussion of this passage, especially in its Markan setting, goes on endlessly without resolution. The kingdom's inauguration in Jesus' ministry is in some sense both revealed and hidden, known and unknown. The Gospel of Mark is noted for its emphasis on the paradox of the manifestation and hiddenness of Christ's identity.[14] Aware of that emphasis, one is less surprised to find the presence of the kingdom characterized in a parallel way. At least for Mark, the cross seems to be crucial for determining both who Jesus really is and his role inaugurating God's rule. In the opinion of some, the secret of the kingdom, like the secret of Christ's divine sonship, is found in his agonizing abandonment in death (e.g., Mark 15:33–39). Ironically, the clue to the kingdom's mystery is found in another mystery! In that God is both revealed and concealed in Christ's death we discover the secret of the kingdom: It is both revealed and hidden in Jesus!

Christians today know a sense of the revealed and hidden presence of God in our world. The paradox that God exercises the divine will in human lives that are still sinful and broken is part of what it means to say the kingdom is both revealed and hidden at the same time. We are never able to claim with confidence that God is reigning in any particular and specific human event. Simultaneously the reign of God is inscrutably discerned and concealed from our discernment. God's dominion is like stumbling in the light with a community that now sees God's present work and now does not see it. We are rightly cautious about saying, "Look, here it is!" or "There it is!" (Luke 17:21). The kingdom of God is not here or there, for it is revealed and hidden at the same time.

Sought or Given? The Jesus of the Synoptic Gospels invites us to seek God's reign in our world. In contrast to an anxious preoccupation with food, drink, and clothing, Jesus urges us to "strive first for the kingdom of God and his righteousness, and all these things shall be given you as well" (Matt. 6:24–33; see also Luke 12:22–31). Associated with seeking God's dominion is storing "up for yourselves treasures in heaven" (Matt. 6:20; see also Luke 12:33–34). The "gate" to the kingdom is narrow and its entrance achieved only by the most committed (Matt. 7:13–14).

On at least two different occasions inquirers confront Jesus with the question of what one must do to gain eternal life (an expression associated with the kingdom). In one case a wealthy man is told to sell his possessions and give the profits to the poor (Mark 10:17–22//Matt. 19:16–22//Luke 18:18–23). The second occasion involves the lawyer who is told to love God and his neighbor but who then asks who his neighbor might be. Jesus responds with the parable of the good Samaritan (Luke 10:25–37). In a similar story in Mark (12:28–34), when a scribe affirms the commandments to love God and neighbor, Jesus says he is "not far from the kingdom of God" (see also Matt. 22:34–38 and Luke 10:25–28).

What all these passages have in common is the radical demand placed on those who would become part of God's new rule. The impression is that life in the kingdom requires a drastic transformation. Indeed, the righteousness of those who enter the kingdom must exceed even the current models of righteousness (Matt. 5:20).

But Luke surprises us with another of Jesus' sayings: "Do not be afraid, little flock, for it is your Father's good pleasure *to give you the kingdom*" (Luke 12:32). Luke sandwiches this startling promise between two sayings that stress the radical demands for qualification to enter the kingdom: Strive for it above all else (Luke 12:31) and sell your possessions in favor of treasures in heaven (Luke 12:33).[15]

Other passages may also imply that the kingdom is a gift to humans rather than a life we earn through our commitment. The kingdom "belongs" to children and those who enter it must become like children (Mark 10:14–15//Matt. 19:14//Luke 18:16–17; see also Matt. 18:1–5). That provocative saying, interestingly enough, is butted up against the story of the wealthy ruler who is told to sell his possessions and give to the poor (Mark 10:17–22//Matt. 19:16–22//Luke 18:18–23). The parable of the workers in the vineyard seems to make a comparable point. The workers are hired to labor in the vineyard at various periods in the day, but at the end of the workday they all receive a payment for a full day's work. The employer defends his decision by appealing to his freedom to do as he choose with what belongs to him (Matt. 20:1–16). Entering the kingdom depends on God's generosity, not our own labor.

Even the Gospel of John expresses something of the same paradox concerning earning and being given the kingdom. The Johannine Jesus seldom speaks of the moral demands made of believers. But at times he says the all-important indwelling of God and Christ with them (see chapter 4) requires obedience. For instance, Jesus says that, if out of their love believers "keep (his) commandments" or "words," the Spirit will come to the community (John 14:15–16), he and God will make their "home" with the community (John 14:23), and they will "abide" in Christ's love (John 15:10). On the other hand, on the one occasion the Fourth Gospel uses the phrase "the kingdom of God," the message seems to be very different. Nicodemus can "see" and "enter" the kingdom only if he is "born from above" (or "born again"). But that new birth depends entirely on the mysterious work of the Spirit, who, like the wind, "blows where it chooses" (John 3:1–9). Being born from above is not something we do for ourselves; it is done to us. Entering the kingdom depends entirely on God's free work, even though life with God, Christ, and the Spirit demands faithful obedience.

The new reign of God is, on the one hand, a gift given out of God's own generosity and mercy; on the other hand, it is a radically new life humans must wholeheartedly seek. If we are honest with the gospels, each of those formulations is true, but neither is true without its relationship with the other. Another paradoxical feature of God's dominion.

Conclusion. This mysterious new reign of God initiated in Jesus' ministry, death, and resurrection defies simple explanation and description. No wonder the disciples sometimes were confused and misunderstood their teacher. In itself the kingdom is a provocative metaphor that pulls at our imaginations and evades our comprehension. Its advent is fraught with paradox. It is now but not yet, revealed but hidden, given and yet sought.

To live in the kingdom is to dwell in an enigma, to be denied easy understanding, and to be propelled in quest of the mysterious. Life in the new rule of God leaves us stumbling in the light, but like children we follow God's voice in Christ. We dare not pretend that we understand or know, but only trust and keep on seeking understanding in the broken world. The Synoptic Gospels further the search with another group of Jesus' teachings.

Pictures of the Kingdom

Probably no group of gospel passages are more treasured, yet more controversial than Jesus' parables. The Synoptic Gospels consistently put those parables in the context of the kingdom of God. That setting is sometimes immediate when Jesus introduces a parable with "the kingdom of God is like," or "is as if," or "may be compared with…" (e.g., Mark 4:26, 30; Matt. 13:24, 31, 33, 44, 45, 47, 18:23; and Luke 13:18, 20). Even when a parable is not explicitly introduced as comparable to the kingdom, many scholars argue the context of the kingdom is implicit in the Synoptics themselves. After a general introduction to the metaphorical character of the parables, this discussion will concentrate on only two examples of Jesus' provocative stories as pictures of the kingdom.

Parables as Metaphors. The word parable itself is the English transliteration of the Greek *parabolēn*, which literally means to "throw alongside." The word is used to speak of an assortment of figurative sayings much like those the Old Testament calls *mashalim* (e.g., proverbs, riddles, and wise sayings). The Hebrew word seems to mean literally "to be like." Bernard Brandon Scott defines a parable as "a *mashal* that employs a short narrative fiction to reference a transcendent symbol." In the case of Jesus' parables that symbol is the kingdom of God.[16]

The parables attributed to Jesus in the Synoptic Gospels are of various sorts, but the ones that concern us are a few of the narrative parables, that is, those that comprise a short story. Compare, for instance, the figurative saying in Matthew 6:22–23 with the tiny story in 13:44. In the latter one hears a tale, a plot unfolds. Many of the best known of Jesus parables are narratives (e.g., the good Samaritan and the prodigal son, Luke 10:30–37 and 15:11–32). In these narrative parables the story functions in a sense as metaphor.[17] The story is juxtaposed with something else so as to create a relationship between the story's plot and that other reality. Sometimes the story seems clearly to become an attribute of the kingdom (e.g., Matt. 13:44). Sometimes the story is associated with a situation. The Pharisees and scribes are grumbling about Jesus' free association with tax collectors and sinners, so Jesus tells three stories about losing and finding (Luke 15). The topic of conversation in Matthew 11:7–15 is John the baptizer, so the reader naturally takes the story of children playing in the marketplace (Matt. 11:16–17) as having something to do with John and Jesus.

Still, like good metaphors, the parables often leave us a bit puzzled. Some are straightforward in their influence on a topic (e.g., Matt. 18:21–35). A number of others stir our curiosity with the ambiguity of their "meaning." The most we can do in those cases is to leave the parable open and let it work on our imaginations while we discuss it with others. For instance, Jesus sets alongside the kingdom a story about the farmer planting seed and then awaiting its growth (Mark 4:26–29). The story is simple enough, but what has it to do with the kingdom? Is Jesus suggesting the kingdom grows mysteriously like the seed? Or, does the story hint at the importance of acting for the kingdom at certain times (sowing and harvesting) and trusting God's actions at other times (between the sowing and harvesting)? In some such way, the story ignites new reflection on the kingdom.

The provocative parables sometimes create their ambiguity by details of the story. Parables are frequently rather commonplace stories (e.g., being robbed on a lonely road or losing a precious coin). But the most puzzling of them have some slight twist in the narrative, in a character's speech, or perhaps in something that goes unsaid. Those narrative bits or gaps are frequently the sense in which the story becomes something more than a simple everyday occurrence, and by means of which the story shocks us, especially in relationship with its context. For instance, the potential uncleanness of leaven hidden in flour teases us (Matt. 13:33//Luke 13:20–21). Is the kingdom unclean?

Like every metaphor, the narrative parable metaphors are both like and unlike their subject. The dissimilarities are as important as the similarities, so that the "is" and the "is not" of the relationship is important.[18] (See the discussion of metaphor in chapter 2.) Like any good metaphor, it is also a mistake to close a parable's meaning rather than allowing its ambiguities gradually to reform our perspective. For instance, rather than reducing the parable of the good Samaritan (Luke 10:30–37) to a simple lesson, we live with it. Gradually it changes our view of relationships with others. The parables are most often metaphors put into dynamic interchange with another metaphor, the kingdom of God. Consequently, each influences the meaning of the other. Charles Hedrick has proposed that the parables are poetic fictions and that their vision of reality challenges our own horizons of perception. The only way to allow them to work in our lives is to leave them open without authoritarian interpretation and to become participants in the stories themselves.[19] Through narratives, parables do what good metaphors always do.

Kingdom Justice. Two parables are good examples of the metaphoric quality of Jesus' stories. They exemplify how the dynamic between the kingdom and the story subverts our sense of certainty and compels us to search for new understanding. In a sense, both may have to do with justice, but certainly, too, with much more.

The first parable is most often called the *laborers in the vineyard* (Matt. 20:1–16), but it might well be entitled "the generous employer."[20] It comes toward the end of Matthew's story of Jesus' ministry. The immediate context is Jesus' promise that devotion to him will have its rewards. But there may be some surprises in those rewards, as the last verse before the parable suggests (Matt. 19:28–30).

The story is a simple account of a farmer's hiring idle workers to labor in his vineyard. Five times he finds unemployed persons in the market and hires them on, each at a later period in the workday. At the end of the day he settles up with them and pays each for a full day's work. When the group that began work in the early morning sees the latecomers being paid a full day's wage, they assume they will receive more. When they receive the same amount, they dispute the farmer's action. It seems unjust to them that those who worked only one hour should receive as much as they who have labored through the heat of the day. The parable closes with the farmer's defense, in which he says three things. First, he has fulfilled his contract with the disgruntled laborers. Second, it is his choice to pay all the workers the same wage. Third, he raises two questions to the discontented workers: "Am I not allowed to do what I choose with what belongs to me? Or are you envious because I am generous?" (Matt. 20:15). The last words of the parable echo 19:30: "So the last will be first, and the first will be last" (Matt. 20:16).

Jesus begins this story with the invitation to relate it to the kingdom (20:1). The realism of the narrative includes the likelihood of vast unemployment in Palestine in the first century. Throughout the workday there are still individuals in the marketplace hoping to hire out for a few hours (20:4–8). Verse 4 suggests the employer makes a general contract with the workers hired at nine o'clock and apparently does the same with those who begin at noon and at three o'clock ("he did the same"—20:5). However, nothing is said about wages to the last group hired at five o'clock (20:7). The payment is made "beginning with the last and then going to the first" (20:8). The words "first" and "last" (*prōtoi* and *eschatoi*) link the story with both its prefatory word (19:30) and the attached saying at its conclusion (20:16). The story then hangs in the frame of the saying about the first being last and the last first, and verse 8 internally connects the tale with its frame.

Verse 9 is the story's turning point. To our shock these who have worked only one hour receive a day's wages. The word translated "grumbled" in verse 11 (*goggyzo*) is the same one used to describe the religious leaders' displeasure at Jesus' association with those held to be sinners (e.g., Luke 5:30; 15:2; and 19:7). It also appears in the Greek translation of the Old Testament in connection with the displeasure of the people of Israel during their time in the wilderness after the exodus from Egypt (e.g., Ex. 16:2 and 8). With the decision to pay all the workers a full day's wage, the story suddenly takes on a different mood. If one has been attracted to this employer for his persistence in recruiting the unemployed, now his actions puzzle us and lead us to question the wisdom of his decision. We easily identify with the grumblers and their sense of indignation. An injustice has been done them, no matter what the farmer had agreed to pay those who came later to the job (see 20:4–5).

How is this story like (or unlike) the kingdom? Its fictional world challenges our fundamental sense of justice and shakes our confidence in divine justice (if this is what God's justice in the new reign is like).[21] This parable, linked as it is with the kingdom, seems particularly strange in the Gospel of Matthew. Jesus' words in this gospel clearly stress the divine reward for righteousness and the dire consequences of unfaithfulness. Remember, for instance, the refrain promising God's secret reward for secret piety (6:4, 6, 18) and the "outer darkness where there will be weeping and gnashing of teeth" (8:12; 13:42, 50; 22:13; 24:51; 25:30). This gospel seems to teach a strict sense of divine justice. However, the gospel's text rather subtly recasts that impression.[22] First comes this parable—one readers will find only in the Gospel of Matthew—and with this parable we hear for the first time in this gospel that the first and last will be reversed. Then as Jesus' final public teaching, Matthew's gospel presents the scene of the last judgment (25:31–46). We are not surprised that the text promises such a judgment. What surprises us is that the righteous did not know they had aided Christ when they aided needy humans ("the least of these who are members of my family"—25:40). The righteous have done their righteous deeds without awareness of what they were doing!

The destabilizing of a strict and calculated divine justice is not entirely dissonant with the Matthean Jesus. The parable of the generous employer is part of a subplot of Matthew. This shocking, even embarrassing story undermines our sense of justice and disorients us. It speaks of a reversal not unlike those we encountered in the Lukan material (see chapter 3). Oddly enough God's restoration of justice is one thing we expect of the renewal of divine rule in our world, but this parable frustrates any effort to impose our own sense of justice on God. It sends us in search of what God's justice may be like. We stumble along in the light!

The troublesome parable of *the dishonest manager* (Luke 16:1–8) does not help us much. Here is a story of a rogue who at least seems to get rewarded for his dishonesty. The parable's context is not immediately enlightening. Chapter 15 contains the three parables of the lost and found, and ends with the father's plea to his elder son to celebrate his brother's return. The first puzzle of the parable of the dishonest manager is whether it somehow connects with the previous three parables and their setting (Luke 15:1–2). Should we read the story of the roguish manager in the context of that nasty older brother and his unwillingness to share his father's joy in the younger son's return? Those questions haunt us as we read Luke 16:1–8. So also does the story's ending trouble us. It trails off with a number of isolated sayings that seem to be a kind of miscellaneous collection of lessons that might be drawn from the parable (16:8b–9). Actually interpreters argue over where the parable itself ends and a commentary on it begins—verse 8a or 8b? Likewise, 16:10–13 might also be construed as an interpretation of the parable. Clearly the parable leads us to consider material wealth and faithfulness.

Without clarification from its context and with no reference to the kingdom (as is the case with Matt. 20:1–16), we are left with little less than the tale itself, making it that much more baffling. The manager is charged with wasting his employer's goods and is in effect told to clean out his desk and leave (16:1–2). Verses 3–4 take us inside the manager's private thoughts. If we had hopes that he might repent of his dishonesty, we are disappointed. We hear only his desperation. He has no other options, so he devises an ingenious but risky course of action. Systematically he discounts the accounts of his debtors (16:5–7). At this point we are denied a vital piece of information—the first of several gaps in the story. Are the discounts he so freely gives customers coming out of his own commission or his boss's profits? We don't know. Even without knowing, the news in verse 8a comes as a total surprise: "And his master commended the dishonest manager because he had acted shrewdly." Here is another gap: Does the word dishonest refer to the manager's initial "squandering" of his boss's property or to his reduction of customers' bills? If verses 8b–9 are part of the parable—and we are not sure they are—they tell us only two things: (1) People of the world are better trained in shrewdness than are religious folk, and (2) we should make use of money for more significant purposes. Neither entirely solves the puzzle of the parable.

The parable's story takes two successive and surprising turns. The first comes with the manager's decisive and drastic actions in verses 5–7. He has just been fired, considers his options, acts, and by story's end is called in to receive a commendation. He reverses his destiny through decisive but precarious action. Just how his actions are successful is not clear. The story's most startling turn comes with the employer's commendation of him for what he has done. Does the master commend this conniving scoundrel for sacrificing his commission to get his boss paid by these deadbeat creditors?[23] Or, is he commended for acting decisively and with ingenuity? Either way, this is a story about a scheming, sneaky fellow who takes control of his own destiny and turns it around. The parable's shock comes in two stages—one with the manager's action and the other with the employer's praise. Part of the puzzle of the parable involves which of these constitute the story's climax. Or, is it both together? But the story's last line still calls him "dishonest."

What is this story designed to do? What does it have to do with the kingdom of God? Interpreters have proposed a variety of readings of this baffling story.[24] The evangelist clearly links the perplexing parable with the Christian's use of material wealth. If verse 8a comprises the story's conclusion, as I think it does, then Luke seems to have attached a number of sayings related to wealth. That is one of Luke's favorite themes and surely a viable reading of the parable that we should take seriously. But it may be only one among many sparks of thought fired off by this story, all of which ought to be considered in dealing with such a provocative and shocking picture of the kingdom. Again kingdom justice is not what we would expect it to be. To start with, the story's hero is a crook, yet his story is worth telling in the context of the kingdom. Did Jesus intend to shock his hearers with a dishonest hero, much as he shocked them by making a Samaritan the hero of another parable (Luke 10:25–37)? But further and deeper, the tale suggests that decisive and shrewd actions are commendable even in the context of God's new rule. Again things are not what we expected them to be in this dominion. Justice has a different flavor.

Bernard Brandon Scott provides a fresh reading of this parable. He proposes that justice is linked in the story with power and vulnerability. The employer first uses his power over the manager by dismissing him. But the manager's actions make him even more vulnerable to his employer's power. He lays himself open to new and more serious charges. In a surprising twist, the rich man responds by himself becoming vulnerable. By commending his employee's shrewdness, he abandons his power and stands side by side with his inferior manager. Scott's offers this summary of his provocative interpretation of the story:

> When the master's praise and the steward's behavior clash with the justice implied in the kingdom (i.e., when story and kingdom expectations collide), the hearer must reconsider what justice in the kingdom can mean. The parable does not redefine justice…(It) breaks the bond between power and justice. … (and) equates justice and vulnerability. The hearer in the world of the kingdom must establish new coordinates for power, justice, and vulnerability. The kingdom is for the vulnerable, for masters and stewards who do not get even.[25]

If we elder siblings accept the invitation to celebrate our brother's return, we find ourselves at a party where justice and power are redefined and we share the vulnerability God demonstrated on the cross. Indeed, this was the elder son's problem in the parable preceding the story of the dishonest manager (Luke 15:11–32). His father's invitation to celebrate his brother's return challenges the elder son's strict sense of justice and threatens the power he had gained through his faithful service. The cheating and conniving steward, the most unlikely of characters, demonstrates a vulnerability the elder son lacks. More strikingly, the rich man relinquishes his power and strict sense of justice to commend his employee.

If we allow it to do so, Jesus' story of the dishonest manager works gradually on our consciousness to corrupt our assumptions about God's justice, power, and status. The placement of this story in the context of the kingdom creates friction that threatens to scorch our visions of what we think God's rule should be. Furthermore, when we take both of these narrative pictures of kingdom justice together, any arrogance we may have about knowing God's ways begins to erode. Actually, networking these two parables with the root metaphor of the kingdom of God leaves us a good deal to discover. In the first of our pictures of the kingdom it is the empowered owner who acts decisively and surprisingly to redefine justice. In the second, it is the steward, the lowly hired clerk, who takes the lead role and pioneers a new way of seeing justice, power, and vulnerability. Finally, however, we have no other option than to leave these two parables open, to admit that we must go on discovering new surprises in them for our lives together as Christ's body. We cannot close their possibilities for meaning, since we do not fully understand them. However, one thing is clear: They teach us we have a great deal to learn about justice, power, and love.

Conclusions: Living with the Kingdom

The kingdom of God is a metaphor fraught with tensions and ambiguities,[26] so much so that we probably do not really know what we ask for when we habitually pray, "your kingdom come." Whatever God's rule in our world is, we do not fully understand it, cannot always identify it when we see it, and most clearly cannot program it to meet our needs. When you link such a rich and varied metaphor as the kingdom with the narrative metaphors of the parables like the two we have discussed, you get a recipe for searching, learning, and discovery.

The Synoptic Gospels report that Jesus sometimes ended provocative and important statements with the injunction, "Let anyone with ears to hear listen!" (e.g., Mark 4:9; Matt. 11:15; Luke 14:35). It is an invitation to open hearing, attentive appropriation, and willing consideration. Those words acknowledge that we do not have to hear; we can "turn a deaf ear" to words that we would really rather not hear. Might it be that the church often would rather not hear Jesus' voice when it shakes our certainty or disturbs our security? To hear with openness the disturbing sounds of the kingdom invading our world involves our willingness to have our perspectives altered. It entails a daring acceptance of a new vision of reality.

The church is a community of faith stumbling in the light because it is not our kingdom we seek. So long as we acknowledge that God is more than our puny definitions and that the divine will is as mysterious as the wind, we will be glad to admit we are still in lots of ways "in the dark." God is the light, but we do not have control of the divine light on a dimmer switch. "Stumbling in the light" is a metaphor for all that we do not know, understand, or recognize. To admit we stumble admits our frailty and affirms our eagerness to learn and to be led along to the light of a new day.

Reaching for the Light

In a sense, our efforts to understand God's kingdom and to interpret the parables for our lives are gropes for light. But in this section the image of reaching for the light speaks of a dimension of Christian theology (that is, our efforts to think clearly about our beliefs). In particular, this discussion will consider Paul's language in terms of its metaphoric qualities and suggest that it represents the apostle's search for understanding. We perhaps sometimes claim more for our theology than is appropriate. The church rightly tries to assess the possibilities of change on the basis of its theology. But to do so requires that we first have a clear understanding of the limits of our theological formulations. In no way does this minimize the importance of theology. Quite the contrary, theology is the way in which faith most often seeks understanding. The goal is really to explore what it might mean for us to take seriously the metaphorical quality of much (if not all) of the language we use to express the content of our faith.

In order to accomplish its goal, this section first inquires about the role of metaphor in theological discourse. Second, it examines the metaphorical character of Paul's theological language, which is the basis of many of the church's doctrines. Finally, a brief concluding subsection asks what all this means for the community of faith, stumbling as it does in the light.

Our Faith Is Like...

On its surface the metaphorical quality of much of our Christian language is obvious. As Jesus himself did, we speak of God as Father. In effect what we do is to put side by side the reality of the mysterious and eternal God and our earthly human experience of a father. The metaphorical quality of calling God Father is evident, and it depends on our having an experience of a father. Suppose, for instance, a young person's experience with her father is negative, and she knows only a brutal and abusive father. How can she speak of God as Father? For her the metaphor may not suggest the caring divine nurturer originally intended by the title Father.

But the metaphorical quality of our theological language is equally evident in other ways. We speak of Christ as God's son and our brother; and we use "children of God" to name our identity in relationship with God and Christ. Each of these continues the practice of putting familial experience alongside transcendent and divine matters. When we talk about the Bible as the word of God, we play with a mental image of God as one who speaks words as we humans do.[27] Even to commune with God is to suggest that our relationship with God is somehow like the relationships we have with people.

It is relatively simple to identify pieces of our common religious language that have the characteristics of metaphors. We can readily see that we put divine, transcendent, otherworldly subjects into provocative relationships with our earthly, human experiences. Upon reflection it is also easy to understand why we do this. We have no other language with which to speak of that which transcends our lives and our world. How else could we speak of God and Christ and our relationship with them without resorting to metaphor? It is much like our efforts to identify and speak of our identity; we can either resort to poetic and imaginative language or remain silent.[28]

The problem is not that we speak metaphorically. The problem is that we do not always acknowledge what it is we are doing. The use of such expressions as those I have mentioned above has become so commonplace for most of us that we do not readily recognize their metaphorical quality. To use Paul Ricoeur's language again, the metaphors are "dead." That is, we give them a clear and unequivocal meaning and forget their metaphorical quality. One of the many contributions of feminist theology has been to shake us out of our slumbering use of metaphors for God. The assault on the masculine character of most of our Christian language awakens us to the simple facts that much of it is metaphorical and that men created and have controlled those metaphors through the church's history.[29] Not coincidentally, the feminist discussion of our religious language has accompanied a new recognition of the role of metaphor in theological discourse. Theological positions on the matter vary, as do understandings of metaphor and its role in theological language. But Sallie McFague claims, among other things, that metaphor is necessary in theology because "we have no alternative but to recognize personal, relational language as the most appropriate language about God."[30]

Something precious is lost when we are numb to the metaphorical character of our language and when we have deadened our metaphors. We lose the sense that there is both a similarity and a dissimilarity between the two realms we bring together to talk of God and our faith. If, for instance, we simply equate God with Father without consciousness that we are using father as a metaphor, we become unaware that God both is and is not Father. When metaphors are used unconsciously, they lose their original provocativeness, shock, and surprise. But perhaps most important, if we remain unaware of the metaphorical nature of our faith statements, we fail to understand our own language. To slay our religious metaphors is to forget that we express our beliefs in a language stretched beyond ordinary, daily language. We forfeit a sense that we are trying to speak of the transcendent. Consciousness of the metaphorical (or poetic) quality of our theological expressions assures an awareness of God's otherness and protects against our domestication of the divine.[31]

Claiming to Know and Not Having Knowledge

The apostle Paul was aware of the role of metaphor in language that speaks of Christian belief. He was a Jew born, raised, and probably educated—at least in his early years—in the Hellenistic world. His language shows evidence of a conscious use of the rhetorical skills of his day.[32] Surely metaphor (as it was understood in that culture) was one of the skills Paul brought to his writing and speaking.

A reading of his epistles convinces one that Paul often used explicit metaphor in communicating the nascent faith to young Christians. Several examples of his use of figurative comparisons come to mind. Romans 11 attempts to shape a healthy understanding of the relationship between Jews and Gentiles in the Christian church at Rome. In addressing the Gentiles, Paul speaks of them as "a wild olive shoot" grafted on to an olive tree. As such they could not "boast over the branches" (11:17–18). His point is that they are graciously added to God's plan of redemption for the world.[33] Two other examples are found in Galatians. In 4:21–31 Paul calls his discussion of Hagar and Sarah an "allegory" (*allēgoreō*). In this case Hagar and Sarah each stand for something specific (i.e., slave and free), and Paul is arguing for Christian freedom. Earlier in the same epistle Paul uses an "example from daily life" (literally, "speak in a human way"—Gal. 3:15). In order to show God's promise is still valid, he puts the promise God made to Abraham side by side with a person's ratified will (3:17–18).

Paul knew how to bring common and well-known experiences from daily life and relate them with matters of the Christian faith. In a more profound way Steven Kraftchick has proposed that Paul metaphorically associated God's act in Christ with Christian moral life. Kraftchick studies Paul's use of the hymn in Philippians 2:6–11 (which summarizes Christ's story) to stimulate Christian behavior among the epistle's readers. He presents a convincing argument that Paul places Christ's lordship in metaphorical relationship with ethical behavior and does so without reducing the theme of the hymn to moral admonition. "Existence in Christ," he concludes, "is given order and structure by the metaphorical mapping of the hymn's structure onto the Christian life." His provocative essay suggests the role of metaphor in Pauline thought as a whole.[34]

Paul's Context and Task. Paul explicitly used metaphorical language and more subtly in Philippians metaphorically linked the Christ hymn to Christian behavior. It should not surprise us then to learn that his theological language in general makes ample use of metaphor. This is particularly evident in the way in which metaphor appears in Paul's efforts to articulate what he believes God did in Christ for humankind.

Paul is often trying to articulate the benefits of God's act in Christ and defending it against misunderstandings. He had little or no precedent for this task. At least to our knowledge, he was one of the pioneers in the effort to think through and make a case for human salvation in Christ. To be sure, Paul stood with one foot on the shoulder of the Hebraic and Jewish heritage and the other on a Christian tradition passed on to him. His use of the Old Testament and Jewish thought is clear. He also clearly and explicitly acknowledges a Christian tradition at a number of points (e.g., 1 Cor. 15:3; see also 7:10 and 12). It appears that he knew creeds and liturgical hymns, which we think originated in the church before him (e.g., Phil. 2:5–11; Col. 1:15–20; and perhaps Rom. 1:3–5).[35] Notwithstanding his resources, Paul was still forging new understandings of the Christian faith. Moreover, Paul was in the forefront of the church's missionary movement into the Hellenistic world. Consequently he was among the first major proponents of the claim that God's work in Christ was for the benefit of Gentiles as well as Jews. In some cases, he had to defend his understanding of the gospel message against campaigns of other Christian missionaries (e.g., see Galatians), but he was convinced that Gentiles were equal partners in Christ and that the gospel message included them.[36]

Paul was in a sense, then, improvising as he went along. We are sometimes tempted to think that Paul was the first systematic theologian of the church. In fact, however, he was far more of an applied theologian or, better, a mission developer who did theological reflection out of practical and concrete situations. He articulated the faith as he understood it for specific congregations with specific problems and issues. Even Romans, perhaps his most systematic epistle, seems to have a specific agenda for that church (i.e., the relationship of Gentile and Jewish Christians—see Romans 1:18—3:20 and 11:1–36). Paul's theological statements, therefore, are not alone for the sake of cultivating "right doctrine" but more often for providing motivation and sanction for specific behavior. In many ways it is wrong to look to Paul for absolute and unswerving theological consistency.

All of this is important when it comes to considering Paul's theology. Without a full manual of Christian doctrine on which to draw and with the well-being and growth of the churches foremost in his mind, he fashioned his theology as he went along. In a sense, Paul too was stumbling in the light, and his theological statements are inquiries for the sake of understanding.

Metaphor in Pauline Theology. In this context Paul employs metaphor to articulate his emerging understanding of the benefits of Christ's death and resurrection. As early as 1950 Eric H. Wahlstrom expressed this clearly in his introduction to Pauline thought. For Wahlstrom, Paul's main issue was the relationship between God and humans, and the apostle's task was to articulate how that relationship is altered by Christ. To accomplish that task Paul used "picture language" (which Wahlstrom also explicitly calls "metaphors"). In order to show the transformation of the relationship between humans and God, Paul drew from a wide range of daily experiences to speak metaphorically of what God accomplishes in Christ for humans. So, for instance, from the practice of slavery in his day, Paul drew his use of the terms redeem and redemption. We were slaves but have been made free in Christ, much as a slave's freedom might be purchased.[37]

A few additional examples will suffice. One case is Paul's use of reconciliation. In Romans 5:10 Paul declares that we were "enemies" of God but in Christ have been "reconciled to God." In 2 Corinthians 5:18–20 he announces that God has "reconciled himself to us through Christ, and has given us the ministry of reconciliation."[38] Paul places two fields of experience side by side. The one is our knowledge of broken, alienated relationships. We know the experience of being enemies with another and then having the relationship changed and the enmity overcome. Paul uses our knowledge of such an experience to enlighten what God accomplishes through Christ. To use Kraftchick's words, the known field "maps" the unknown field for us. The vague sense that Christ has changed our relations with God "is given order and structure by the metaphorical mapping" of the domain of human brokenness and enmity.

Another example entails Paul's use of adoption as an image of what God does for humans through Christ. He uses the word in only two passages—Romans 8:23 and Galatians 4:5. In the second of these the apostle says "God sent his Son ... so that we might receive adoption as children." In the Romans passage the adoption is something the Christian awaits in God's future act for us.[39] The language imagines us orphans (or slaves—Gal. 4:7) who are formally made God's children through Christ. Again, a human social event is put into relationship with a divine event in order to open insights into the latter.

A final and more difficult example is Paul's use of the verb justify. This is more difficult because justify and justification in Paul are such hotly debated issues in some quarters of the church. Moreover, there is clearly a Hebraic-Jewish background for the concept of divine justification.[40] Still, it provides another kind of metaphor Paul evokes. The verb (justify) and/or its noun (justification) appear in two of Paul's letters—Romans (2:13; 3:4–28; 4:2–5; and 5:16) and Galatians (2:21). Basically, the metaphor is drawn from the experience of being accused of a crime, tried for it, and acquitted. That experience, Paul claims, helps us understand what God has done in Christ for us. It "maps" our wrong before God but also declares exoneration of us. Paul makes clear, however, that our justification comes as a result not of our innocence, but of God's "righteousness" and "grace" (Rom. 3:21–24; Gal. 2:21).

One further observation about Paul's use of these metaphors is important. Again and again, we find him "mixing his metaphors," that is, putting them into relation with one another. Galatians 4:4–7 successively refers to redeem, adoption, child, and heir. Romans 3:24–26 weaves together justify, redeem, and atone. (The latter draws on Jewish sacrificial worship for its field of reference.) Romans 5:1 links justify with having peace (the cessation of warfare). In these cases Paul constructs a network of metaphors, each of which seeks the same goal, but he allows these metaphors to bounce off of one another. In passages such as these, we are given the relationship of each metaphor's origin in experience to its meaning for our status with God, but the richness of each individual metaphor is deepened as it is interpreted by the other metaphors. For instance, what does it mean for us to be purchased from slavery (redeemed) and at the same time declared acquitted of our offense (justified)?

With such language Paul probes the still-uncharted relationship of humans with God as a result of Christ's cross and resurrection. His goal is to elucidate that new relationship (see 2 Cor. 5:17—"new creation," another metaphor). Each metaphor spotlights a single aspect of the Christian's life with God, but to press these metaphors too hard for their conceptional differences may be ill-advised. For instance, we cannot make too much of the difference between justification and reconciliation, except to say that they picture the results of Christ's work for us in different ways.

Paul's Metaphorical Language

In 1 Corinthians 8:2–3 Paul writes, "Anyone who claims to know something does not yet have the necessary knowledge; but anyone who loves God is known by him." These words introduce his effort to resolve a conflict among the Corinthians over eating meat that has been sacrificed to idols. Some in the Corinthian church claim to know whether such a practice is proper. But those words are also a good description of Paul's theological endeavors. Paul knows the gospel message; witness, for instance, his passion in Galatians 3:1–5; 4:9; 5:1 and 12. He "loves God" and knows that he "is known by" God. But his language suggests that Paul does not claim to know exactly all there is to know about how God has transformed the human condition in Christ. Instead, he stretches out in search of understanding, for he believes there is something new and important out there. Metaphor is his means of searching. By trying this metaphor, then that one, and by putting them together in new and provocative combinations, his probes become flashlight beams into the mysterious and unknown.

Paul's theological language is filled with metaphors. It is well for us to allow his language to continue to work metaphorically. Sometimes we are tempted to harden Paul's images into descriptive language—to give them precise meanings in our theological dictionary. This is helpful in some ways but costly in others. We should continue to cling to Paul's ideas as the basis of our own understanding of the faith. We should also continue to recognize their metaphorical, poetic, and probing characteristics. If we do so, those metaphors will prove richer. They will continue to spawn new ideas and—equally important—new and contemporary metaphors. Paul's metaphors can help us continue our stumbling quest for greater understanding.

Conclusions

This discussion has attempted to demonstrate a single point in both Jesus' proclamation of God's kingdom and Paul's statements about Christ's work: Metaphors make provocative and paradoxical declarations for faith seeking understanding. While there may be a knowledge in faith itself, there is also a realm of the mysterious and unknown for us to try to understand as best we can. Since we cannot claim to know all there is to know, we speak with poetic and figurative language. That language points us to truth, wraps truth in paradox, and leads us through our ignorance.

The paradoxical stance of the church is that it claims to know and embrace something fundamental to its existence, while still having to grope in the confusion of change for understanding. We accept the gift of God's reign among us without fully understanding what that rule is, but in faith we claim it is both present and coming. We know that in Christ we have been brought into a new relationship with God, but we can only speak of that relationship with metaphors drawn from our experience in this world. In this sense we are a community of faith on the way home, but stumbling in the light.

It remains to review the metaphor of stumbling in the light. That will entail summarizing some of the tensions the discussions of Jesus and Paul have uncovered. Finally, this conclusion evaluates the usefulness of this metaphor.

Unifying the Image and Its Tensions

The passages we have examined suggest some components that comprise the metaphor of the church's stumbling in the light.

Jesus' Proclamation of the Kingdom. Jesus never offers a definition of God's new reign beginning in his ministry. Instead he allows the rich and traditional image of God's exercise of the divine will in the world to spark expectations and entice hearers. His words about the kingdom are filled with paradox and enigma. It is present or near at hand but at the same time still to come, revealed but still shrouded in mystery, and both sought and given.

With his parables Jesus provides stories that purport to be pictures of life in this novel kingdom, but the stories themselves are sometimes filled with ambiguity and puzzles. Those who have ears to hear them must struggle with their meaning and what they tell us about the kingdom. In many cases they challenge our assumptions about how God would rule this world and force us to seek new understanding. Justice, power, and vulnerability seem to have new meaning and significance in the kingdom, but we are never certain of how these are redefined in God's dominion. So, we go on struggling with the parables, allowing them to ignite new insights and gradually to transform our view of reality.

While we accept God's gift of the divine reign and commit ourselves wholeheartedly to it, its mystery remains. The Christian walk is clouded by that mystery. Following Christ into the kingdom means being forever learners; it means always leaning forward to meet what may surprise and even shock us. However, we stumble on in the light of the kingdom's mystery, trusting the one who invites us there.

Paul's Reaching for the Light. Paul is a traveler with us into the kingdom Christ inaugurated. He models for us what it means for faith to seek understanding of things too great for human comprehension, but he has learned from Jesus. As Jesus centered his proclamation in a metaphor and used metaphorical stories to stimulate search for the meaning of the kingdom, Paul uses metaphors to express his understanding of life in Christ.

Paul filled his letters with a variety of metaphorical pictures of what God accomplished through Christ for humanity. With images of justification, redemption, adoption, and many others, he probes the mystery of what he does not know in its entirety. As a result, what we know of his theology is really a collection of those metaphors. When we or Paul bring these images together, they interact with one another to produce new meaning and further metaphorical expressions. That interaction is filled with wonder and enigma. God treats us as if we are orphans seeking a home; but also, as a divine, gracious, and righteous judge, God acquits us of the wrong that is ours. God buys our freedom as if we are slaves, but at the same time treats us as enemies to be reconciled with their Creator. Tensions permeate the relationships within the configuration of the images of Paul's thought. Indeed, through Paul we learn better to recognize the frequency of such imagistic language in our declarations of faith. Paul sensitizes us to the nature of articulations of Christian beliefs.

Together Paul and Jesus demonstrate the role of metaphorical language in speaking of what God does in our world. They both present the advent of God's new relationship with humans in enigmatic ways that suggest the mystery of God's presence and activity. Since God's thoughts and ways are not our thoughts and ways (Isa. 55:8), we can never fully understand life with God under the divine will. We are led toward understanding with probes of the mystery.

The Merits of the Image

The discussions of Jesus' proclamation of the kingdom and Paul's metaphorical theology lead us to the image of the church's stumbling in the light. The distortion of the world in which the church lives makes God's work in Christ appear all the more mysterious and incomprehensible. The distortion is not just around us; it is in us. It images our own finiteness, the limitations of our understanding, and our propensity to impose our own ways onto God. The light with which God illumines us and the world has not yet overpowered our creaturehood. The church has tried to speak of this fact with what has been called "original sin." Through that doctrine the church endeavored to acknowledge the simple fact that we inherit and perpetuate the condition of a world alienated from its Creator, even when in faith we embrace God's redemption of us from that condition.

Therefore, the image of the church's stumbling in the light is important for us. It suggests that we are still residents of a sinful world and experience that sinfulness within us. The image provides us a way of confessing our continued participation in sin, alienation, and brokenness. The church needs healing and redemption and does not pretend to be pure. Indeed, together we find healing with one another through the word and sacraments God has given us. The image of the church's stumbling character also sobers our claims to knowledge. If ever we are tempted to claim to know what we do not know, the image of stumbling helps us toward a realistic humility. Like Paul, we know the gospel message: In love God has sought us out and claimed us for the kingdom. But knowing that, we can then confess that there is much that we do not know.

A church that seeks to deal creatively with change needs to be realistic about itself. We need to acknowledge our own sinfulness and lack of understanding. Only then can we openly consider the possibilities of change and assess their degree of faithfulness. An arrogant church is never open to change, but one that is humble will have to ask if change is for the better. The church in North America is currently in the throes of assessing the possibilities of gay, lesbian, and bisexual persons within its ranks and whether such persons should serve in the church's clergy. Congregations that understand themselves to be stumbling in the light receive those questions with a degree of openness. We ask if we really know the status of such persons before God. Do we really know the biblical views of homosexuality as they relate to contemporary gay, lesbian, and bisexual lifestyles? If there is sin and brokenness among the gay and lesbian communities of our society, is it really any different from that which is characteristic of all Christians?

A church that conceives itself stumbling in the light has a different attitude toward change. Jesus suggested that his listeners would experience drastic change in the kingdom of God. Change, therefore, always offers the possibility of discovering a new dimension of life in God's dominion that has heretofore been undiscovered. What we seek for the contemporary church is only that: A willingness to consider the possibilities of change. With that kind of attitude in a congregation, genuine discussion of change is possible. Together we can seek to discern whether the Spirit is at work in any proposed change.

Of course, like every metaphor, there are dangers inherent in conceiving of the church as stumbling in the light. The greatest danger is that it will dim our commitment to the heart of the gospel message. That is why the metaphor must be glued to that of a community of faith. Our faith is the basis of our search for understanding, and without faith there would be nothing to understand. Stumbling pictures the understanding we seek and not the faith out of which we live. The essential gospel message anchors our quest for understanding

Thinking of ourselves as stumbling in the light can also paralyze us, making us fearful of error. We can so emphasize the church's stumbling gait that it overpowers any confidence that we can learn together. As a Christian community, we can become so afraid of making errors in our judgments that we will be unable to come to decisions. Congregations need a healthy dose of humility about themselves, but true humility arises from a realistic assessment of oneself and—more important—of what God can do with us. We stumble together in the light confident that God is with us on the way. That confidence yields the possibility of discerning God's leadership and of making clear and faithful choices.

So, the church is then both like and unlike a community of faith stumbling in the light. As with every metaphor, there is a similarity and dissimilarity between the church's life together and stumbling in the light. Faithful use of this image entails exploration of both the likenesses and differences it suggests. We never forget that the church is not like a community stumbling and about to fall, for it has seen the light of Christ. But at the same time, we are ever conscious of the limitations of our understanding and our need to be led toward the light.

How do we do that? How do we use this image of stumbling in the light, along with the other two metaphors constructed in chapter 3 and chapter 4? How do we effectively cultivate these images of a congregation's self-understanding? Our agenda for the last chapter is full!

CHAPTER SIX

Sowing the Seeds

Seed planting is a long-term investment and a statement of confidence in the future. When we sow seeds, we commit ourselves to a long period of patient waiting. We know it will take time for tiny seeds to grow into plants. Planting seeds of new congregational self-understanding is no less a matter of patience and perseverance. It entails a long-term ministry and willingness to labor tirelessly before any results are discernible. But visionary pastors are accustomed to this kind of ministry and undertake the process for the sake of the church's future.

The central metaphor for a new self-understanding is now complete. The results of examinations of selected portions of the New Testament have yielded a single sentence: *"The church is a community of faith on the way home stumbling in the light."* To construct this one statement, the translation of New Testament themes employed three discrete metaphors for the church—on the way, homing, and stumbling in the light. Along the way, cases have been made for the potential each individual metaphor has for enabling the church to deal more creatively with change. Further questions still remain. How might this general metaphor facilitate a self-understanding that empowers us to deal more constructively with change? If it seems that the metaphor has such potential, how can we employ it in congregational ministries in ways that help us conceive of change as integral to the church's life?

The goal of this final chapter is to present strategies for implanting and nurturing new images for a congregation's self-understanding. However, before turning to those specific strategies, the discussion needs to review the total metaphorical sentence. So, the first section attempts that review and raises some questions about the image. The second section then asks about the process of implanting and nurturing new self-identity in a congregation.

The Metaphor in Review

The thesis is that the metaphor, "The church is a community of faith on the way home stumbling in the light," holds promise for helping congregations think differently about themselves so that they are better able to engage questions of change in healthy and creative ways. The translation of both explicit and implicit biblical images of the church scattered throughout the New Testament, however, holds problems as well as promise.

Empowering Christians for Change

Empowerment. Asking if the metaphor empowers congregations to deal with change brings us face to face with two difficult questions: How do we empower others? What constitutes empowerment? There is something mysterious about the process of empowering others. In spite of all the analyses of empowerment proposed today, few if any of us fully understand the process.[1] Sometimes our best efforts at enabling persons to think and act differently seem to produce little or nothing. Then, when we are least hopeful that some sermon or program will succeed, we are liable to learn that it was effective, that some found new strength in our efforts. Sermons are a good example. The ones I work the hardest to prepare are frequently met with yawns. Then the one I am least proud of solicits meaningful expressions of gratitude.

So, we need to honestly recognize at the beginning of an evaluation of the metaphor for self-understanding that we cannot "program" empowerment. That is the case, I suspect, for at least two reasons. The first is the complexity of human personality. People respond to the church's ministry out of their very personal situations and in terms of their individual personalities. Furthermore, our ministries may not always have the effect we design into them for the simple reason that we are dealing with human consciousness. Empowerment comprises changing consciousness—that elusive sense people have of themselves and the world around them. To endow others with a capacity to deal with change is to tinker with that basic human awareness. That is not easily done, as any one who has done some pastoral counseling knows all too well. Another reason we cannot predict the results of any effort of ministry is due to God's freedom to use or not use our efforts. In other words, the results of a ministry designed to evoke new congregational self-understanding invariably depends on the work of the Holy Spirit in and through our human efforts. That is, of course, equally true of the whole of our ministries.

Nonetheless, we are called to do our best with what we have to offer. So, the possibilities of this study's metaphor must be scrutinized. That scrutiny leads us through three overlapping features of the metaphor.

Becoming. The metaphor of the church as a community moving toward its destination and struggling with uncertainty speaks of the people of God in a process. It is commonplace to speak of individual life and maturation as a process.[2] Some might even say that a person is an entirely different individual over the course of time; there is hardly a single ego that sustains continuity in the process. This is no less the case with a community. Certainly a perusal of the history of any North American denomination demonstrates a process of becoming. A congregation's history is little different.

The metaphor tries to express that process, raise it into consciousness, and give it a positive connotation (i.e., on the way home). Our image of the community tries to capture the language of process scattered throughout the earliest church's understanding and experience. What it endeavors is to entice one into a recognition of the reality of change and progression that is at the heart of the church. If you picture the community of faith on the way home stumbling in the light, you are brought inside a becoming as well as a being. The church is becoming something each moment of its existence. It is never stagnant but always dynamic.

The problems with implanting such a process of becoming in the communal consciousness of a congregation are innumerable. Humans prefer being to becoming. Parishioners have their fill of process in their individual lives, their families, and their work. They don't want to hear about their church's becoming. On the other hand, this is also the very strength of the metaphor. Just because we know how pervasive process is, we can understand our identity as a church in those terms. Those of us who want to sow the seeds of the church as a community in the process of becoming appeal to that sense that change permeates the whole of life.

If we can help people think of the church in a process of becoming, they will want to deal with change in a different way. In a sense, process is inevitable. But, if we believe that institutions and individuals are more than simple products of their environment, we believe too that we can influence the process of becoming. That makes it necessary to ask in what ways do we choose to change. What change is fitting and which is unsuitable for the church? If a congregation can think of itself as on the way, involved in process, it will engage change with a readiness to exercise faithful wisdom. In dealing with a question of change, we acknowledge that whatever we decide is going to contribute to what it is we are becoming. If we decide to remain with the old hymnal, for instance, the process moves in one direction; if we adopt the new hymnal, we proceed in a different direction. In effect we are saying that change is going to happen to us with any decision we make. The dynamic quality of human existence as a whole makes that inescapable. The church is always becoming something!

Instability. However, process and becoming imply instability. If the metaphor we are evaluating does anything, it fosters a degree of instability in a congregation. The word instability, of course, is loaded with negative connotations. We speak of emotionally disturbed persons as unstable. Congregations said to be unstable are often those that are experiencing problems. To argue that there is an inherent instability in being the people of God in our world is disconcerting to say the least. On the other hand, instability also expresses a willingness to grow, to become. To be stable implies being static; to be unstable suggests dynamism. Children are unstable when they take their first steps, but that is part of their process of learning to walk. Congregations that admit and live an instability are those that recognize they are on the way and learning along the way. They confess that the Christian community is their home but acknowledge another sense in which they are stumbling along, seeking their divine home.

Furthermore, there are forms of instability that arise from basic stability. The buildings that are made to survive earthquakes have a structural instability or flexibility that allows them to move with the shifting of the earth on which they stand. Deeply rooted trees exemplify stability, but the instability of their limbs allows them to withstand powerful winds. The instability of the church is rooted in the stability of God's call. So, the congregation can change; it can shift with cultural changes because its roots are deeper than any one culture.

Finally, instability, like process, is inherently part of human life. We recognize the instability (or vulnerability) of our individual lives, of the society of which we are part, and now even of the entire planet on which we live. Insecurity is intrinsic to existence, especially in our day. So, the metaphor once again invites us to think of the church in terms of what we know to be characteristic of our whole lives.

The church in the twenty-first century knows the experience of instability. To emphasize that feature calls on the congregation to deal with the possibility of change as part of the pervading presence of instability. The major metaphor of this study tries to put instability and change into a tensive relationship with stability and permanence. We are a community of faith that knows it has a divinely created home, and we stumble along a path that has been illumined by God's light. The metaphorical similarity and dissimilarity are paramount. As a church on the way, we live with an instability born out of our firm foundation in Christ. So, we welcome change as part of our lives together and as an opportunity to make conscious decisions about our future.

Authority. The three chapters on New Testament passages stress the church's need to learn. The church experiences "surprises along the way," knows and does not know its home, and searches for truth. What it knows in faith is always held in tension with what it does not know. Probably this lack of knowledge contributes the most to the process and the instability that the metaphor nurtures, but the suggestion that the church lacks knowledge is doubtless the most offensive feature of the image this study proposes. I have already tried to articulate that offense, especially in the last chapter. More needs still to be said with regard to the authority that God has granted the church. That authority is found especially in the truth of the biblical witness and in the institutional features of the church derived from scripture.

Is *the Bible* not our certain source of knowledge? Does it not eliminate our ignorance? A full treatment of the authority of church calls for another book, perhaps many books.[3] Nonetheless, it is important to acknowledge some of the difficulties that arise from viewing scripture as our source of knowledge.

First, the variety of the interpretations of scripture vividly demonstrates our lack of knowledge. We do not know how the Bible is to be read and understood; that is part of our stumbling journey. Claims for the absolute knowledge found in scripture are based on views of biblical authority and interpretative techniques that are not universally embraced. The variety of views of its authority and interpretation epitomizes our quest for understanding. Shifts in those views represent the church's instability and its process of becoming. We must confess that as a whole body we are not certain of how scripture is authoritative and how it is to be read in order to put its authority into practice.[4]

Beyond that awful reality is another. Scripture simply does not answer all our questions. It offers us its own paradoxes and mysteries. Which of the several biblical views of suffering, for instance, should we embrace? In addition, the Bible is silent when it comes to many of the most important issues facing the church today. It has nothing at least directly to say on abortion, genetic engineering, cloning, or space exploration. We can mine its basic teachings for principles on which to construct Christian views of such issues, but there too we stumble in the light. Which teachings shall we elevate to the status of principle?[5] The authority of the Bible resides elsewhere. The living word of God assures us of the possibility of a loving relationship with our Creator and of the promise of God's continued presence and guidance, but it does not entirely annihilate the uncertainties of our lives and world.

The church also treasures *practices and beliefs arising from scripture*, which have become part of its institution. They are a portion of what we claim to know for sure. For example, in various ways the church values the so-called office of the keys, most especially the forgiveness of sin. The church is granted authority to forgive sins in the name of Christ (Matt. 16:17–19). The sacraments of holy communion and baptism are still other precious bits of confident knowledge. Does the picture of the church as a community lacking knowledge undermine the authority of such practices?

Again we need only witness the variety of ways in which such institutionalized practices of the church have been interpreted. The authority to absolve sin is interpreted and practiced in remarkably varied ways. At one extreme such authority is vested exclusively in the church's clergy. At the other extreme some practice that authority by simply reading passages of scriptures having to do with God's forgiveness. The practice of the sacraments is equally splintered, so much so that it is a paramount issue in all ecumenical discussions. We know God forgives sins; we know God has given us sacramental means of appropriating divine grace, but how they are to be put into practice and how they are true and effective remain questions we cannot seem to resolve satisfactorily together.

To speak of the church's lack of knowledge is to recognize the uncertainties that plague us even when we would rather not do so. In a sense, the metaphor constructed out of New Testament language dares us to acknowledge the obvious. That may mean conceding that our denominational heritage does not have a corner on the market of truth. It may mean confessing that our congregation practices the authority of its faith in one way but not necessarily the only Christian way.[6] As disconcerting as such acknowledgment of lack of understanding of authority may be, it is profoundly biblical and strangely empowering. With a consciousness of our endless quest for understanding, we view change in a new way. Change may offer us fresh ways of probing the unknown and experiencing surprises along the way. To repeat the theme discussed in the previous chapter, a congregation that knows that it does not know has a different posture toward change. Our congregations are in desperate need of a basis on which to engage in serious discussion of crucial matters.

Our society is becoming increasingly divided on some significant issues and unable to talk with one another about them. The voices for each side of every issue seem to become more and more shrill, and there is less and less willingness to listen to the voices on the other side. The church has an opportunity to serve our society's common welfare by becoming a safe place to discuss controversial issues. We are a community that can acknowledge that absolute certainty is not ready at hand in some matters. We can become a community that models the search for understanding for the sake of our whole culture. Within such a community of faith the views of all sides can be honored, heard, and debated. The church has an opportunity to exercise a new kind of authority—the authority to be a forum in which our society can seek understanding.

Such a promise as this is implicit in the self-understanding nurtured by the metaphor before us. We can be a community that meets the possibilities of change with open arms, because we believe we have something yet to learn about life and goodness. The metaphor promises becoming, instability, and authority only within lack of knowledge. All three have potential for empowering consciousness for change, but not without additional problems.

Facing the Problems

The problems that accompany the promise of the metaphor are at least two. Consideration of these two leads us closer to the question of how we foster new metaphors for self-understanding. Both involve the nature of metaphor itself.

Momentary Insight. A metaphor is, as we have observed, a creative, momentary occurrence of language (see chapter 2). A metaphor affords us a flash of insight, the power of which resides in the moment of its hearing or reading. That moment passes as quickly as it comes, and we are back in the humdrum world of ordinary language.

How then can the metaphor of the church as a community of faith on the way home stumbling in the light function effectively? Once you have heard it, its poetic power is drained. The shock is over and gone. If we engage our congregation in a study of this metaphor and preach bits and pieces of it, will it have any power beyond its introduction? The question really implicates all of our uses of metaphor for communal self-understanding, whether it be the one this study advocates or others.

Worn Out. The second problem is like the first. Even if the metaphor is a promising one, the more we use it, the more common it becomes, the more likely the possibility that we will wear it out. We have already done that to some of our images for the church's self-understanding. I recently worshiped with a congregation on a Sunday as they celebrated an infant's baptism. Hanging behind the baptismal font was a small banner on which were the infant's name, a baptismal symbol, and the words "You are a child of God." It represents a marvelous feature of this congregation's regular practice of baptism. But then I thought to myself how thinly worn is that expression "child of God" (at least in my denomination). We have used it so much that it has nearly become a cliché without meaning.

Rich metaphors, however, resist wear. They go on interminably provoking new insights. Still, the richest of metaphors will wear thin, particularly in our current culture. We have become a society that prefers literal language and consequently tend to deaden the provocativeness of our symbols and metaphors with simple definitions.

Even the best of the images for the church's self-understanding will evoke insights as only momentary flashes and will wear out with continued use. How then can the metaphor of this study or any other help us over the long haul in the fostering of new self-understanding for change?

Stimulating New Metaphors. Earlier the discussion suggested that metaphor stimulates other metaphors. The flash of insight offered by one rich metaphor results in other provocative associations of language. Our Christian expressions are filled with such offsprings of metaphor. That Israel is called "children of God" generated a countless number of metaphors down to our own day; for example, we are orphans seeking parents.

It may be that the stimulation of other metaphors is all we can expect of this study's general metaphor. In itself it may serve only a short-term purpose in shaping congregational consciousness around a new identity. It may even provide reasonable wear before it grows commonplace, but in the long run its usefulness may be found in the other metaphors it evokes from you and from members of your congregation. The metaphors of this book may do little more than turn a congregation's attention to neglected features of its self-images. In my experience, the metaphors I use in teaching or preaching are helpful. But on the occasion of one of my better efforts, there will always be at least one student or one parishioner who will come up with a variation on my metaphorical expression or an entirely new image that arose from mine. In a sense, good preaching and teaching entail this practice of using metaphor to excite metaphor. Among the best sermons I have heard are those in which the preacher wove her or his own image in response to the language of the biblical text. John's image of the light shining in the darkness (John 1:5) provoked one preacher to speak of our "night lights." The beast of Revelation excited another preacher to explore Christian life through the metaphor of "the beauty and the beast."

The first strategy for employing the materials of this book for the cultivation of images of new congregational self-understanding is this: Use the metaphors of this study to stimulate new and different images that empower us to deal with change. The use of this book in your ministries may begin with preaching, teaching, and discussing some of its ideas and language, but its most faithful use will occur in two phases: (1) using the metaphors of this study to stimulate your own imaginative pictures of a corporate self-understanding ready to engage the possibilities of change and, (2) using the metaphors of this study to evoke images in the imaginations of your parishioners. I invite you to trust the power of metaphor to elicit other metaphors.

You, I, and our congregations are not likely to create a metaphor that will serve the church for centuries to come, but together we might excite a congregation to begin a journey toward a new identity. If the church is a community on the way, engaged in a process of becoming, using its instability to learn and its lack of knowledge to probe uncertainty, its metaphors, too, will change. Part of what it means for the church to be a dynamic organism is that it will endlessly envision new images of self-understanding for change within change.

This clan of images can work to fashion new self-understanding. Some will not wear long, but others may serve a congregation for a full generation. Still, as the congregation's leader, you are responsible for sowing seeds that sprout and pollinate other plants. Therefore, the images with which you attempt to empower a conscious self-identity equipped to deal with change must be sound as well as stimulating ones. The principal and general task is to speak and write about the church and change so as to liberate the congregation from its fearful paralysis in the presence of new proposals. With that foundation for a strategy in mind, let's become more practical.

Sowing the Seeds of New Self-understanding

This section is designed to offer you, however sketchily, some concrete procedures by which to empower your congregation for change. In the light of all that has just been said about empowering and about metaphor stimulating metaphor, this discussion proceeds through several steps. The first step is making preparation for the sowing of seeds for new self-understanding. The next three steps discuss how those seeds might be sown in preaching, teaching, and discussing.

Preparation for Sowing

Planting always entails preparation. Before beginning the process of implanting the beginnings of new congregational self–understanding, we should consider preparation for sowing. Congregations are often only vaguely aware of their identity as a community of faith and may see no reason for thinking other than they do about themselves. So the preparation for planting new possibilities of self-understanding entails first of all raising consciousness about congregational identity. It involves turning the soil of present consciousness over, so that it can receive a new seeding. Sometimes one has to tear down in order to build up. Jeremiah was commissioned "to pluck up and to pull down, to destroy and to overthrow, to build and to plant" (Jer. 1:10). The pastor of a congregation may have to engage in plowing under some current images of the church to make way for new seeds. This can be done gently, in love, and with appropriate humility. Pastors can creatively play the roles of the inquisitor, analyst, and critic of prevailing notions of the congregation's self-understanding. These roles are most authentic and effective, I believe, when the pastor publicly subjects her or his own views of the church to the same scrutiny.

Pastors have three goals in this early stage. The first is to bring views of congregational identity into the light of day. If we often operate without full consciousness of corporate identity, the task is to invite people to pull those images out of the recesses of their minds. The second goal is to evaluate, question, and sometimes challenge the adequacy of many of the images with which we live our communal lives.

The third goal may be more difficult: to nurture a consciousness of the both-and quality of Christian knowledge. In the language of this study, the pastor is likely the one who sees and names the paradoxical and tensive character of views of the church. For instance, parishioners might be inclined to stress the community as a place of refuge and peace. The pastor affirms this but puts alongside it the fact that our life together as Christians entails being challenged and our peace disturbed by mission (see, e.g., Matt. 10:34). If you intend to cultivate tensive images of the church's identity in which opposing truths are held together, you need to introduce that quality in this preparatory stage. Contemporary Christians are likely to want single and absolute answers to questions; they may not be prepared to accept both-and answers. Preparing to implant the new seeds requires that you help parishioners discover the paradoxical dimension to Christian faith and life. This is a considerable task, but also one that is biblically and theologically sound as well as supremely practical.

In order to accomplish these goals, one might consider a number of ways by which to prepare the soil for planting:

- Persistently raise the question of "who are we as a congregation?" in sermons, adult studies, and administrative discussions (see below).
- Invite parishioners to think about and share with one another their understandings of the identity and mission of the church both on the congregational level and in terms of the church as a whole. Acknowledge that the congregation's self-identity is composed of the people's views, and encourage them to take ownership of the issue.
- Challenge people to assess their understandings of the congregation's identity. Model such assessments by offering critical insights into popular notions. Most of all, you should challenge ones of which you yourself are fond; for instance, "we are a family." Try placing such images in tension with others; for instance, "we are a broken family." This is best done in a dialogical setting, such as an adult

study. Or, a sermon might challenge some cherished view a congregation holds of itself. Small-group discussions of that sermon might follow the congregation's hearing it.

- Use biblical material in sermons, adult studies, and devotions for administrative meetings that begin to probe the issue of corporate identity. What does it mean, for instance, that the Hebrew people came to think of themselves as God's possession (e.g., Ex. 19:5)? Model how one needs to evaluate the current usefulness of such a image. For instance, the image of believers as God's children arose from God's possession of the people. But today we do not think of children as possessions.

- Introduce paradox in sermons and studies. Suggest the role it plays in our theology and self-understanding. For example, Christians are simultaneously saints and sinners.

- Congregations are increasingly formulating and using mission statements. You might use the occasion of the formulation or revision of such a statement as a time to stress the importance of communal self-understanding and to evoke discussion of such self-understanding in the congregation.

In some such ways as these you can prepare a congregation to begin the journey toward new images of self-understanding. Pastors can help make people ready to consider new and provocative metaphors for the church.

Preaching New Images

The Role of Sermons. Preaching occupies a precarious place in the church's ministry today. On the one hand, the sermon seems odd when compared with most contemporary forms of communication. The sermon may be the only occasion on which most of your parishioners sit passively and listen to one single presentation of any sort—without visual images continually flashing before them; without the benefit of different voices and faces speaking; without the anonymous, individual attention television viewing affords. The sermon strikes many as quaint.[7]

On the other hand, the sermon may also be the only occasion on which most clergy have the opportunity to communicate with at least a sizable segment of the congregation. This may not be the case in your setting, but in many congregations people are less and less likely to be present for other gatherings. They restrict their participation in the congregation's life to attendance at Sunday morning worship—and sometimes even that only rarely. Sorry, but they will not be present for the adult Bible study, the congregational annual meeting, or the potluck supper and program. Sunday morning worship is the one opportunity you may have to influence their lives. As quaint as it may seem to some, the sermon is a precious means of speaking with your congregation.

Consequently, preaching on texts that have relevance for the congregation's self-understanding is an essential strategy for nurturing new identity. Sermons may provide the best opportunities for planting those seeds of new congregational identity. Another scenario may also fit your situation. Many marginal members of a congregation secretly question the value of the church. These are people who have a vague sense that the church is a good thing and that one ought to support the church, if only superficially. Baby Boomers are coming back to church, we are told, for the sake of their children, while they themselves may still harbor serious doubts about the church and its role in our culture. The soil in these cases may be ready for planting! Addressing the question of a congregation's nature and function may tune in to a frequency of thought and feeling many of your worshipers know all too well.

Sermons come in a variety of forms, but this book is premised on the conviction that the resources for fashioning new images of the church are found in scripture. For that reason it is important that sermons lead worshipers into a text and provoke them to think about their congregation in terms of the earliest Christian communities. This does not eliminate the possibility of the so-called topical sermon. Such sermons can be biblical in the way they treat the topic of communal self-understanding. Whatever the sermon's form, the sprouts of new self-understanding should, I believe, arise from scripture.

Examples. A couple of examples are in order. One passage that occurs frequently in the Revised Common Lectionary, as well as others, is *Peter's famous confession* at Caesarea Philippi, followed by Jesus' prediction of his passion and Peter's response. That story is found in Matthew 16:13–23 and Mark 8:27–33 (see also Luke 9:18–22 and John 6:67–71). Matthew, Mark, and Luke each set Jesus' first words about his death and resurrection in relationship with Peter's confession that Jesus is the Messiah. Mark and Matthew (but not Luke) have a third component to this narrative. Peter "rebukes" Jesus for speaking of his dying, and then Jesus reciprocates and "rebukes" Peter, even calling him "Satan" (Mark 8:32–33; Matt. 16:22–23). He says that Peter is "setting his mind not on divine things but on human things."[8]

How interesting that Peter should be portrayed this way—first in a positive light, then in a negative one. In Matthew's version of the first scene Jesus even calls Peter "blessed" for naming his master Messiah; Peter has received a special revelation of insight (Matt. 16:17). But in the second scene Jesus calls Peter "Satan." What a shocking and provocative contrast those two scenes produce when one follows the other.

But let's not too quickly blame Peter or explain his rebuke of Jesus by appealing to the disciple's fickleness. Matthew is right that Peter's confession that Jesus is the Christ constitutes the church's foundation (Matt. 16:18–19). But we may resist identifying with Peter's refusal to accept Jesus' prediction of his passion. Might the words about Peter's "setting his mind not on divine things but on human things" apply equally to the church?

A sermon might paint this contrast in Peter and then ask if it is not typical of our life together. Like Peter, we hang between perceiving God's revelation in Christ and still having things our way. Revelation evokes our affirmation of faith, but our minds are still entangled in "human things" so that we cannot comprehend our Lord's death as a revelation of God. We see the light of revelation but then, like Peter, we stumble in that light. We both know and do not know, believe yet do not understand. How are we as a church still like the two-sided character of Peter? When we face the possibilities of change, are we always able to discern the things of God and those of humans?[9]

Thomas (John 20:19–29) is another character who may represent an aspect of our lives as a community of faith on the way home, stumbling in the light. The risen Christ appears to his disciples in Thomas' absence (John 20:19–23). When they share their good news with Thomas, he is dubious about it all and insists that he must experience the risen Christ firsthand before he will believe (20:25). The story continues with another appearance of the risen Christ. He addresses Thomas' doubt and makes a believer out of the formerly dubious disciple. Then Jesus speaks these provocative words to him: "Have you believed because you have seen me? Blessed are those who have not seen and yet have come to believe" (20:28–29).

The passage is rich with meaning and a variety of messages for the church today. A homiletical focus on Thomas might, however, be appropriate for a church in the throes of new self-definition. Let's recognize ourselves in Thomas. Who among us has not had doubts about the resurrection? And naturally so, since it defies our understanding of life and death. Thomas is no freak disciple. We are all like him in some ways, or at least sometime in our Christian journey. Doubt constitutes a natural human response to God's act in Christ, and many of us carry fragments of such doubt with us.

Several important features of this Johannine story, however, may help us see our doubts in new ways. First, the living Christ comes to Thomas in his doubt. Doubts do not scare the risen Christ off, nor do they bar us from access to the divine. It may be doubt that occasions our most meaningful encounters with God.[10] Second, it is instructive that the fourth evangelist ascribes to this doubter the highest and most insightful affirmation of Christ's identity—"Lord" and "God" (20:28—see also 1:1). The story parallels the one about Peter but in reverse. Peter the confessor is also the Satan; Thomas the doubter is also the most insightful confessor.

A third insight into this passage is the most important for us. The beatitude in John 20:29 intrigues us. Thomas is granted a special encounter with the risen Christ as a basis for his faith. He "sees." But Christ says to him that the "blessed" ones are those "who have not seen and yet have come to believe." In a sense Christ speaks of those of us who are never granted the privilege Thomas receives of seeing the risen Lord for himself. Christ speaks of us who have come to believe on the basis of the word transmitted to us through others.[11] So, the church is a community that has come to believe without seeing (in the strict sense of that word). Like Thomas we all yearn to see for ourselves (see John 4:41–42). Being a community walking by faith, we are then careful about what we claim to have seen. We grapple with the uncertainties of the world around us and within us to understand, to see. But that dilemma is far from tragic! Christ calls it "blessed!" Our blessing is in the risk of believing and the search for understanding that faith motivates. God's love and acceptance of us is not qualified because we believe without seeing. Quite the opposite.

As children, we learn that sometimes we obey the boundaries our parents set on our behavior without understanding the reasons for those boundaries, but we trust our parents' care for us and obey. Like children, we believe without understanding because we trust God's care for us. As a church, we go on seeking understanding, hoping to see more than we have. Consequently, we are ready to consider a variety of ideas and proposals for truth because, having not seen, we are eager to learn God's truth for us and our world.

A different kind of sermon might be constructed on *Paul's admonition* in Romans 15:7: "Welcome one another, therefore, just as Christ has welcomed you, for the glory of God." The passage goes on to make it clear that Paul is speaking to Jewish Christians ("the circumcised") about welcoming Gentiles into their community (15:8–12). Setting the text in a historical perspective proves helpful. First-century Jews were inclined to despise Gentiles. They regarded Gentiles as unclean and thought their moral lives were disgusting. The word Gentile is sometimes even used in the New Testament in a pejorative way (e.g., Matt. 5:47; 18:17). The ways of Gentiles were abhorrent, then, to the Jews who became Christians. For that reason some early Christians insisted that Gentiles must first become Jews before being admitted to the Christian community (e.g., see Gal. 2:12). They insisted Gentiles must be circumcised and obey Jewish law before they qualified for Christian baptism. (See the discussion of Acts in chapter 3.)

Paul admonishes us to welcome others who are different from us as Christ has welcomed us. That places us in a terrible dilemma. We have our standards of Christian morality and believe the church stands for a certain lifestyle. How then can we welcome those whose morality is not "up to our standards?" Do we not compromise the church's purity by admitting those we regard as immoral? In this way our dilemma is much like that of the early church.

Yet, are we really so certain of our own morality? Is it possible that there are a variety of lifestyles that could be called Christian? What we are sure of is that Christ accepted us. With all our impurities, all our immoralities, Christ includes us among God's children. So, perhaps we should welcome others (about whose morality we have doubts) just as Christ has welcomed us. We are certain of God's accepting love in Christ. That certainty, and not a moral standard, is the foundation of our life together. Our identity as a church is not found in our common morality; it is found in our common faith that Christ welcomes us as we are. Gathered around that faith, we struggle together to learn what it means to live our faith in the difficult decisions of life.

(An index of biblical citations in this book is found in its last pages. It may help you isolate portions of the discussion that might stimulate reflection for other sermons that address a congregation's image of itself.)

Intentional Preaching. Our three examples suggest how biblical texts may afford us avenues into the questions of the church's self-identity. However, preaching to empower a congregation to deal with change in healthy and productive ways requires careful planning. Every sermon cannot be turned into an occasion to address congregational self-understanding. That would prove to be unfaithful to the biblical texts and terribly predictable. Better, the preacher ought to plan sermons in such a way as to raise the issue on the occasion when appropriate texts are read. It ought to be a recurring theme without becoming a monotonous one. Create a schedule of sermons with a smattering of those designed to address congregational identity.

Certain seasons of the liturgical year are more likely to be appropriate occasions for preaching to empower the church for change. The long season of "ordinary time" (or what is sometimes called the Sundays after Pentecost) is a period in which the liturgical year deals with our Christian life together. The season of the Epiphany is another good time to wrestle with this issue. If you are not a lectionary preacher, or a lectionary preacher not afraid to depart from the lectionary readings, you might want to consider a series of sermons on the church, its identity and mission. For such a series you could use the structure of the book with its three different metaphors, one for each of three sermons. Or, you might devote one sermon to each of the following: Israel as the people of God, the disciples as the first community of faith, the church in Acts, and the church in Paul.[12] If preaching is important in the strategy for nurturing images for new self-understanding, planning one's preaching is vitally important.

Teaching New Images

Preaching new metaphors for the church is important, but so too are opportunities for teaching. The participants in an adult study may not be as numerous as those who sit in the pews on Sunday morning, but such groups often comprise many of a congregation's leaders. To influence and empower a congregation's leadership is important both in the strategy of teaching and what below I call discussing new images. This brief subsection proposes two adult studies as suggestions for approaching the subject of new self-identity for a congregation.

The Church in a Time of Change. The first proposal is for a study of the contemporary church and its cultural setting. The words church and change in the same title might tantalize your parishioners and motivate them to come out at least to learn what you have in mind. Such a study group could take a great many different forms. The following is only one proposal to stimulate your own reflections on such a course for adult parishioners.

The goals of the course are (1) to review the state of the church in a rapidly changing society and (2) to stimulate reflection on how the church should respond to change. Chapter 1 might help you in your preparation. Another useful resource is Robert Wuthnow, *Christianity in the Twenty-First Century: Reflections on the Challenges Ahead* (Oxford: Oxford University Press, 1993).

The following is a proposed structure for the course.

1. *Changes in Our Culture.* In the first session invite the participants to itemize all the changes—for the better and for the worse—they have witnessed in their lifetimes. Encourage them to think about fundamental transitions in our culture. For instance, the ease of communication or the way in which we can no longer think of ourselves as a Christian nation. Allow them to express their fear of such changes and to ventilate their feelings of disappointment in what is happening in the United States today. Your task would be to bring order and insight to the discussion, but you will want to have your own list of changes and observations about our culture to supplement those of the participants.

2. *Changes Confronting the Church.* In this session explore how cultural changes have impacted the church. How have certain changes in our society reached into the church and brought innovation among us (e.g., the women's movement)? Again, the participants will probably want to ventilate their emotions about such changes. Attend to their fears and insecurity. Name the major ways in which cultural change results in changes in the church. Offer your own assessment of these impacts on congregational life and how they have threatened you. Explore how, as the church, we are both part of but

different from our culture, and point out that we are never free of cultural influences.

3. *How Do We Assess Proposals for Change?* In the third session you come to the heart of the matter, namely, the participants' understandings of themselves as the church. You should invite the class to seek the heart and core of what it means for them to be the church. How then does that help us in dealing with proposals for change? You might offer an example as a kind of case study, something from a real situation facing the church. It might, for instance, be the proposal that the congregation have a "contemporary worship service" to supplement the traditional one. Or, it might be a proposal coming from your denominational headquarters. The task is to try to help the class discover what really counts in their life as a Christian community and how their view of change relates to that basic understanding of the church.

4. *Resources for Change.* This session requires you to come prepared to help the class discover some sources of insight and empowerment from scripture and tradition. You might begin by sketching some of the biblical resources for aiding in change. Use chapters 3 through 5 as they are helpful. Show the group how the faith communities of the Bible had to deal with change and how they managed it. Second, from traditions of the whole church, and your denomination in particular, point out the same thing: How the church through the centuries had to change and how it managed change. You might compare your denominational roots with where contemporary congregations of your denomination are today and why those changes have occurred. In conclusion, attempt to reassure the participants that the church through the centuries has again and again found resources for change in its faith.

5. *Our Congregation in the Future.* The concluding session assumes that you have begun to equip the congregation for change. Now offer the class some of your new images for the church in a season of change. If you like, summarize the metaphor "The church is a community of faith on the way home stumbling in the light." But also use your own metaphors for the church's self-identity. Invite the participants to offer their images. Here you might try to show how images of the church are invariably paradoxical. We are both a resurrection people and at the same time frightened by death. In conclusion, suggest that such new images that take change seriously equip and empower the church for the future.

This course proposal attempts an inductive approach to the issue, beginning with the participants' own experience of change and what that means for the church. Such an approach contributes at least two important things: (1) The participants take ownership of the task of dealing with change[13]; (2) they become involved in creating new images for self-understanding that empower them to deal with change.

Biblical Images of the Church. People crave good Bible study, especially if it is immediately relevant to their needs. You might find that planting seeds for new metaphors for the church is best done through inviting the congregation to wrestle with selected portions of scripture. The goals of this course proposal are (1) to engage the participants in the study of certain biblical texts having to do with the nature and role of the church and (2) to enable them to imagine new mental pictures for their congregation. This book offers you a resource for just such a study, especially one focused on the New Testament.

The following is a proposed structure for such a course, which you should adapt to your situation and interests. You could shorten or expand this proposal to fit your needs. Before each session prepare a list of the biblical passages to be discussed, so that the participants can read and study them before coming to class.

1. **The Old Testament: A Journeying People.** Frank R. VanDevelder's book *The Biblical Journey of Faith: The Road of the Sojourner* (Philadelphia: Fortress Press, 1988) provides a good resource for this session. You need to begin by stressing that the people of Israel fashioned a basic understanding of what it means to be the people of God. Our views of the church draw on that Old Testament theme. Select from VanDevelder's discussion the most important passages for the group's reading and discussing (e.g., Genesis 12). Of course, you could spend several sessions on this topic before proceeding to the New Testament.

2. **The Gospel of Luke: Disciples on the Way.** The Christian church takes its origin in those who aligned themselves with Jesus and followed him. Use the material in chapter 3 on Luke but translate it into terms your group can understand. Spend part of the session on the biblical expression "way" and what it means. Select the most important passages discussed in chapter 3 and invite your group to ponder what they mean for a congregation that follows Jesus.

3. **Acts: The Church on the Way.** Acts is vitally important, since it affords us our only glimpse into the earliest church. The discussion of Acts in chapter 3 should put you on to some of the important passages that might be productive for your group. Invite the participants in the study to think about what these passages mean for a congregation that follows the Spirit.

4. **John and the Epistles: The Church's Home.** Introduce the idea that God provides a home for Christians and the process of discerning and moving toward that home. For study choose the most important and the clearest passages treated in chapter 4. In this case, it would

be interesting to ask the group to think about this polarity: The congregation is their home, yet they seek another home in the future. How is each true for them? How do they see the relationship of being at home and still looking for God's home for them in the future? Portions of your worship liturgy might suggest this polarity (e.g., speaking of holy communion a "foretaste of the feast to come"). What does this being at home and looking for a home mean for our understanding of ourselves as a congregation?

5. **Jesus and Paul: Probing the Uncertainties.** This will be the most difficult of the sessions, perhaps for you, most certainly for the participants. Indeed it might be broken into two separate sessions— one on Jesus and one on Paul. Or, perhaps you should devote one session each to the kingdom of God, the parables, and Paul's images of the benefits of Christ. From the discussion in chapter 5 select a number of key passages that will aid your purpose of nurturing thought about the church's identity in the midst of change. Invite the group to think about the mystery of the kingdom of God. Lead them in a comparison of the different metaphors Paul uses and help them see the comparative quality of the apostle's language. Let them assess the image of "stumbling in the light" and offer their own alternatives to it.

6. **Our Congregation: How Do We See Ourselves?** On the basis of your biblical studies allow the group to draw its own conclusions for their congregation. Invite them to play with different images of the church—especially as those images might help them deal creatively with change. You could ask them to write or even draw their pictures of a congregation that faithfully deals with change. Let the different images bounce off one another in discussion. Prepare the image you would like them to consider as they conclude their study.

Final Suggestions. These proposals are but two of many ways you could engage a group of your parishioners in some serious study of the church and change. Whatever you may choose to do in the way of study groups as part of your strategy, I suggest that you try to glean the best of the conclusions from your class's study and circulate those conclusions within the whole congregation. One way of doing this is to write a summary article about the course for publication in the congregation's newsletter. Allow the participants to share their experience in this class with committees and other bodies within the congregation, such as the women's and men's groups. Use the stimulation your participants experienced to stimulate still others. You may need to encourage your participants to use their new insights in their leadership roles in the congregation. This leads us to the third strategy for sowing seeds of new self-understanding in a congregation.

Discussing New Images

In my pastoral experience I often found committee and board meetings to be dull and, more often than not, relatively unproductive. I realize now that my own negligence contributed to that dullness and lack of productivity. Had I been more intentional about my role in these meetings, I could have raised more significant questions and provoked deeper discussion.

Such administrative meetings offer pastors opportunities to help laity think more deeply about their congregation. Often behind or underneath the business at hand there lurks the question of who are we as a community of faith in Christ. Our ministries are more faithful when we are willing to push congregational leaders toward that question. Sometimes they may want to get the business done as quickly as possible so that they can return to their homes. Laity, however, are also hungrier for significant theological discussion than we sometimes give them credit for. I suggest we use the occasion of the conduct of business to inquire about and to offer images of the church in changing times. A few examples of actual situations will demonstrate this possibility.

The Basketball Board. A committee proposed to the congregation's council that a basketball board be constructed in the church parking lot. The little village in which the congregation was located had no real "park" space as such. The village youth would enjoy shooting hoops in the parking lot. But the council was reluctant. They had just replaced the windows on the back side of the building, and those new windows would be perilously close to the proposed basketball board.

The proposal was finally reluctantly approved, but this issue raised the question of how that congregation understood itself. Youth were changing; they no longer came home from school to go to work in the barn or even the fields of the family farm. Change for the youth meant that the congregation needed to change its ministry to the community. How do we think of ourselves as the church in this community? This was an occasion for some serious reflection on our images of the church and whether those images included the realities of change taking place all around us.

Rethinking "Family Night." In the congregation's tradition, the first Sunday of each month was designated "family night." The occasion began with a potluck dinner and included a brief program of some sort. But attendance was dwindling, and only the faithful few (who came to every event at the church) were participating. The pastors wanted only to change the name of that event. They suggested some members of the congregation felt the title excluded them. Few of the single people thought they constituted a "family." Some single parents with children also felt uninvited by the title. Could the occasion simply be called "Congregational Night"?

Again the congregation's governing body was reluctant. The elder member of the group launched into a lengthy history of "Family Night." Others voiced their opinion that it was silly to think of "family" as excluding single people and single parent families. Those who objected to the title of "Family Night" were accused of looking for an excuse for their disinterest in the church.

That was a precious "teaching moment" in the midst of conducting the congregation's business. The pastors needed at that time to raise the issue of who we are as the church. Again the issue evolved around change. There were more and more single and divorced people in the congregation. Moreover, the concept of the family had subtly changed through the years. What image of ourselves do we need to accommodate change in our ministry—even changes as simple as the names we give our programs?

Intergenerational Worship. The new attention given to "family values" is appropriate in our culture, even though some of it may be only political hype. The truth is, however, that Sunday morning worship is often a time for children to be quiet, to draw or color on the bulletin, and not be heard. The worship committee proposed that the congregation institute a practice of making one Sunday morning worship a month intergenerational. The pastors had sketched a plan for a worship service that included the participation of all ages. The regular liturgy assumed that worshipers could read. So the pastors proposed, that on the occasion of these intergenerational services, they would compose simple responses that would be spoken and then repeated by the congregation. The sermon would be a "children's sermon"—the adults always said they got more out of them anyway.

The proposal was adopted and put into practice with relative success. But within two months the worship committee had received complaints. The solemn time of worship and meditation was disturbed by all the children who were present. What should the committee do? It might have invited the complainers to gather in order to voice their views to the committee. Such a session would have provided a forum for the discussion of the church's role. Again things have changed. Children are no longer as compliant as they once were to parental insistence that they sit quietly for one hour in a worship service in which they cannot participant. Children are no longer to be seen but not heard. How do we accommodate this change in our services of worship? Does our image of the church take into account such fundamental changes in its youngest members? This is the issue that should have been raised for the consideration of both the worship committee and those who objected to changes in the congregation's worship practices.

These three examples suggest that ordinary and sometimes mundane matters of committee and board business are opportunities to explore images of the church. A pastor who wishes to empower a congregation to deal better with change finds in such incidents a chance to invite people to think more deeply about their view of the church and change. They are openings into the congregation's consciousness through which we might move in order to plant a seed or two and hope they take root.

Persistence Pays Off

Four strategies for sowing seeds of new self-understanding are available to us: preparing the soil, preaching, teaching, and discussing new images for the church. There are doubtless other methods for the same purpose, but these four provide the framework within which ministry can cultivate the possibility of strengthening the church for the challenge of change.

The task, of course, is a lengthy one. To quote Harriet Mary Crabtree again, new images

> …will take a long time to take root. They will be met with resistance by those whose lives are deeply informed by a cluster of images which they believe to be exhaustive, and they will be hard even for those for whom they are meaningful to actually absorb.[14]

Those who aspire to the role of sower and cultivator of new images for the church's self-identity will equip themselves with persistence and intentionality. Many of the seeds they sow will fall among the rocks or be choked by the weeds of indifference and fear. The ones that do take root will be long in bearing fruit. The sowers may never see the results of their labor. They are enjoined to be patient and trust that persistence pays off.

But persistence requires the companionship of intentionality. The strategies outlined above necessitate (1) that clergy have clear and precise goals in mind and (2) that they plan carefully how the sowing is to be accomplished. Finally, they ought always to keep their goals in mind and avail themselves of every opportunity to drop a seed in a human life. Like persistence, intentionality will in the long run reap a harvest. Like the sower in Jesus' parable, there is a mystery about the growing of the seeds (Mark 4:26–29). In this case, as in all our efforts, we trust that God plays the key role in planting and nurturing the seeds of new congregational self-understanding.

Wisdom and Courage

The task of thinking anew about our images of the nature and function of the church is not one that we would necessarily choose from of the vast curriculum of ministerial tasks. Rather, it has been thrust on us by the nature of the time in which we live. A season of change drags us—perhaps kicking and screaming—into this field of endeavor. We could, of course, stick our heads into the proverbial sand and let the world go by, but our callings as servants of Christ will not allow us to do that. Instead, we prepare the seed, load the planter, and set out to cover the ground with it.

By its very nature the church lives by hope. It is a community whose vision of the future is vital to its very being. Therefore, we have reason for a certain kind of optimism. That confidence is not the same as the popular kind of hopefulness cultivated in some quarters as the power of positive thinking. Instead, it is an optimism rooted in God's promise to the church. Pastors undertake the task of changing the images by which the church lives because we share that steadfast hope in God. We believe that God has an important role for the church in this new century and that grasping that role through imaginative thinking is the faithful response to the divine promise. We plant seeds for new self-understanding in our congregations because we believe God will nurture those seeds into fully grown plants. As a group, Christians are irrevocable optimists! Because it is God's chosen instrument in the world, we have hope for what the church can be in the future.

While on vacation, in the summer of 1930, Harry Emerson Fosdick wrote a hymn that is a prayer addressed to "God of grace and God of glory." At that time Fosdick was embroiled in the turbulent change of the fundamentalist-modernist controversy of the early twentieth century. The hymn was first sung at the opening of Riverside Church in New York City.[15] One of the petitions of that prayer includes this line: "Grant us wisdom, grant us courage for the living of these days."[16]

That petition provides an appropriate conclusion to this study. The "living of these days" with faithfulness and service is possible only with the wisdom and the courage God can grant. The task requires the courage to boldly engage change in new and direct ways, but it equally requires a wisdom that empowers us to respond to change with commitment and steadfast grounding in the good news of the gospel.

May that wisdom and courage be ours in a church amid change.

Notes

Chapter 1: A Season of Change

[1]Philip Rieff, *The Triumph of the Therapeutic: Uses of Faith After Freud* (New York and Evanston: Harper and Row, 1966). William C. Placher has challenged the preoccupation with transcendence in modern religious thought: *The Domestication of Transcendence: How Modern Thinking About God Went Wrong* (Louisville: Westminster John Knox, 1996).

[2]The origins of the magazine *The Christian Century* are rooted in this liberal optimism at the turn of the century. However, the format of the cover was eventually redesigned to emphasize the word century and thereby to defuse the earlier assumption that the twentieth century was destined to be a Christian one.

[3]See, for instance, the work of Paul Sponheim, *Faith and the Other: A Relational Theology* (Minneapolis: Fortress Press, 1993) and more recently Gordon D. Kaufman, *God-Mystery-Diversity: Christian Theology in a Pluralistic World* (Minneapolis: Fortress Press, 1996), and Joseph M. Webb, *Preaching and the Challenge of Pluralism* (St. Louis: Chalice Press, 1998).

[4]In its basic principles, H. Richard Niebuhr's classic study *The Social Sources of Denominationalism* (New York: Henry Holt, 1929) remains a persuasive analysis, even though some descriptive details have shifted through the decades since it was written.

[5]A good number of contemporary Christian theologians have anticipated this change and have explored methods of doing theology in dialogue with other prominent religions. See, for example, Gavin D'Costa, *Theology and Religious Pluralism: The Challenge of Other Religions* (Oxford: Basil Blackwell, 1986); J. A. Dinoia, *The Diversity of Religions: A Christian Perspective* (Washington, D.C.: Catholic University of America Press, 1992); Paul F. Knitter, *No Other Name? A Critical Survey of Christian Attitudes Toward the World Religions* (Maryknoll, N.Y.: Orbis, 1987); and John Hick and Paul Knitter, eds., *The Myth of Christian Uniqueness: Toward a Pluralistic Theology of Religions* (Maryknoll, N.Y.: Orbis, 1987).

[6]Robert G. Hughes and Robert Kysar, *Preaching Doctrine for the 21st Century*, Fortress Resources for Preaching (Minneapolis: Fortress Press, 1997), chap. 1. One of the current responses to the radical secularization of North American culture seems to entail new efforts to claim a transcendent reality amid the secular. An example of such a response is found in Robert W. Funk, *Honest to Jesus: Jesus for a New Millennium*, A Polebridge Press Book (New York: HarperCollins, 1996). By means of a radical construction of the historical Jesus, Funk proposes a contemporary spirituality on the basis of a new concept of transcendence.

[7]Among the many studies of the end of Christendom and the post-Christian era in North America are a theological discussion by Douglas John Hall, *The End of Christendom and the Future of Christianity* (Valley Forge: Trinity International, 1996) and Loren Mead's more practical discussions for the ministry of the church in three books published by the Alban Institute (Bethesda, Maryland): *The Once and Future Church* (1991), *Transforming Congregations for the Future* (1994), and *Five Challenges for the Once and Future Church* (1996).

[8]See the provocative work of Pamela Dickey Young, *Christ in a Post-Christian World: How Can We Believe in Jesus Christ When Those Around Us Believe Differently—or Not at All?* (Minneapolis: Fortress Press, 1995). Young concludes, "The Christian identity that I seek is one that recognizes the interconnectedness of all that is and fosters partnership among all creatures in working toward integrity for all who share the world" (p. 146). Other important contributions include these: Terrence W. Tilley, et al., *Postmodern Theologies: The Challenge of Religious Diversity* (Maryknoll, N.Y.: Orbis Books, 1995), especially chap. 11; David B. Burrell, "God, Religious Pluralism, and Dialogic Encounter," *Reconstructing Christian Theology*, ed. Rebecca S. Chopp and Mark Lewis Taylor (Minneapolis: Fortress Press, 1994), 49–78; and Francis Schüssler Fiorenza, "Christian Redemption Between Colonialism and Pluralism," *Reconstructing Christian Theology*, 269–302.

[9]See, for instance, Bernard Brandon Scott, *Hollywood Dreams and Biblical Stories* (Minneapolis: Fortress Press, 1994), 19–45.

[10]Two insightful analyses of the impact of television on our culture are Neil Postman's *Amusing Ourselves to Death: Public Discourse in the Age of Show Business* (New York: Viking Penguin, 1985) and Gregor T. Goethals, *The Electronic Golden Calf* (Cambridge, Mass.: Cowley Press, 1990).

[11]Ellen Goodman spoke of the phenomenon of "infotainment" in her review of Oliver Stone's movie *JFK* in the Minneapolis *Star Tribune*, January 1991, 12A. Her comment is cited and discussed in connection with television in Michael Rogness, *Preaching to a TV Generation* (Lima, Ohio: CSS Publishing Co., 1994), 16–17.

[12]For a far more optimistic view of the Internet see Tom Koch, *The Message Is the Medium: Online All the Time for Everyone* (Westport, Conn.: Praeger Publishers, 1996).

[13]The literature on postmodernism and its impact is immense in volume. An accessible introduction along with a selected bibliography are found in the first chapter of A. K. M. Adam, *What Is Postmodern Biblical Criticism?* Guides to Biblical Scholarship: New Testament Series (Minneapolis: Fortress, 1995).

[14]On science in the twenty-first century and Christian theology and their relationship with other changes see Nicholas Lash, *The Beginning and the End of "Religion"* (Cambridge: Cambridge University Press, 1996). On the threat of relativism see Richard J. Bernstein, *Beyond Objectivism and Relativism: Science, Hermeneutics, and Praxis* (Philadelphia: University of Pennsylvania Press, 1983). Both issues are discussed in Nancey Murphy's *Beyond Liberalism and Fundamentalism: How Modern and Postmodern Philosophy Set the Theological Agenda*, Rockwell Lecture Series, ed. Werner H. Kelber (Valley Forge, Penn.: Trinity Press International, 1996).

[15]For a careful analysis of the impact of this expression of postmodernism on theology see John E. Thiel, *Nonfoundationalism*, Guides to Theological Inquiry, ed. Kathryn Tanner and Paul Lakeland (Minneapolis: Fortress Press, 1994). Also provocative is Jens Glebe-Möller, "The Possibility of Theology in a Postmodern World," *Studia Theologica* 46 (1992), 29–39. From a womanist perspective Delores S. Williams demonstrates how certain fundamental views of current theological thought exclude African American women. *Sisters in the Wilderness: The Challenge of Womanist God-Talk* (Maryknoll, N.Y.: Orbis Books, 1993).

[16]Adam, *What Is Postmodern Biblical Criticism?*, 17.

[17]For instance, see Rebecca S. Chopp, *The Power to Speak: Feminism, Language, God* (New York: Crossroads, 1991), especially chapter 3 and its notes on pp. 148–153, and the discussion in *Reconstructing Christian Theology*, Rebecca S. Chopp and Mark Lewis Taylor, eds. (Minneapolis, Fortress Press, 1994) of Susan Brooks Thistlewaite and Peter Crafts Hodgson, "The Church, Classism, and Ecclesial Community," 303–325, and James H. Evans, Jr., "Eschatology, White Supremacy, and the Beloved Community," 346–73.

[18]At least two other treatments of how the church might meet the challenges of change are important. The first is Robert Wuthnow, *Christianity in the Twenty-First Century: Reflections on the Challenges Ahead* (Oxford: Oxford University Press, 1993). Wuthnow discusses five categories of challenges facing Christianity: Institutional (including the place of the church in culture), ethical, doctrinal (including pluralism), political, and cultural. He concludes with an optimistic appraisal of the future based on the fact that Christianity has a message of hope. "As the United States embarks on a new century that message will clearly be needed as never before" (p. 217). The second treatment is even more radical: Mike Regele (with Mark Schulz), *Death of the Church. The Church Has a Choice: To Die as a Result of Its Resistance to Change or to Die in Order to Live* (Grand Rapids, Mich.: Zondervan Publishing House, 1996). Radical change, Regele argues, brings the church to a "defining moment" in its history.

[19]For a classic study of the relationship of church and culture and a far more elaborate analysis of that relationship see H. Richard Niebuhr, *Christ and Culture* (New York: Harper, 1951).

[20]James W. Fowler, *Faithful Change: The Personal and Public Challenges of Postmodern Life* (Nashville: Abingdon, 1996), 71–73. Fowler acknowledges his use of the work of William Bridges and his own earlier writings on faith development in this analysis of change.

[21]Margaret A. Farley, *Personal Commitments: Beginning, Keeping, Changing* (New York: HarperCollins, 1990), 57.

Chapter 2: The Method of Metaphor

[1]Maya Angelou, "When I Think about Myself," *Poems* (New York: Bantam Books, 1986), 26.

[2]Martin Heidegger, *Being and Time* (New York: Harper and Row, 1962), 145. More recently Gemma Corradi Fiumara has espoused a dynamic relationship between language

and life and the unity of thought and language. Language is a process by which we constantly and reciprocally interact with experience. *The Metaphorical Process: Connections Between Language and Life* (London: Routledge, 1995), e.g., 7.

[3]Paul Ricoeur has probed the complicated relationship between metaphor and concept. He suggests that metaphor is not part of conceptual thinking but "marks the emergence of such thought" and "creates possibility for new conceptional thought." *Interpretation Theory: Discourse and the Surplus of Meaning* (Fort Worth: Texas Christian University Press, 1979), 57. Hence, metaphor gives birth to concepts. They are derived from a more immediate level of apprehension and articulation of which metaphor is part. See also Ricoeur's study "Metaphor and Philosophical Discourse," *The Rule of Metaphor: Multidisciplinary Studies of the Creation of Meaning in Language*, trans. Robert Czerny, et al. (Toronto, Buffalo, and London: University of Toronto Press, 1977), 256–313, and his article "The Metaphorical Process as Cognition, Imagination, and Feeling," *On Metaphor*, ed. Sheldon Sacks (Chicago and London: University of Chicago Press, 1978), 141–57.

[4]Of course, the role of metaphor in self-understanding is finally more powerful than this. Claudia V. Camp observes that "the problem is not, finally, remembering such statements are metaphors, but remembering that metaphors create us and not the other way around." "Metaphor in Feminist Biblical Interpretation: Theoretical Perspective," *Semeia 61. Women, War and Metaphor: Language and Society in the Study of the Hebrew Bible*, ed.Claudia V. Camp and Carole R. Fontaine (Atlanta: Scholars Press, 1993), 36.

[5]Discussions of advances beyond Aristotle's formative views of metaphor abound, and Paul Ricoeur's work often addresses the relationship between Aristotle and contemporary views. See, for example, *Semeia 4: Paul Ricoeur on Biblical Hermeneutics*, eds., John Dominic Crossan (Missoula: Scholars Press, 1975), 76–77. Another such summary is found in an article by Steven J. Kraftchick in which he proposes Aristotle's legacy has been revised in three significant ways: Metaphor is now understood as a way of cognition, as a means of structuring worldviews, and as integral to understanding. "A Necessary Detour: Paul's Metaphorical Understanding of the Philippian Hymn," *Horizons in Biblical Theology: An International Dialogue* 15, no. 1 (June 1993), 11–22. See also Mark Johnson, "Introduction: Metaphor in the Philosophic Tradition," *Philosophical Perspectives on Metaphor*, ed. Mark Johnson (Minneapolis: University of Minnesota Press, 1981).

[6]On juxtaposing see Eva Feder Kittay, *Metaphor: Its Cognitive Force and Linguistic Structure* (Oxford: Clarendon Press, 1989), 17.

[7]Ricoeur, *Figuring the Sacred: Religion, Narrative, and Imagination*, ed. Mark I. Wallace, trans. David Pellauer (Minneapolis: Fortress Press, 1995), 160–61. Elsewhere he observes that major contemporary critics agree that "Metaphor is a kind of 'attribution,' requiring a 'subject' and a 'modifier.'" *The Rule of Metaphor*, 95.

[8]Paul Ricoeur, "The Metaphorical Process as Cognition, Imagination, and Feeling," 145. Ricoeur also points out that a metaphor creates "surplus of meaning" in the language it uses; the words show themselves to mean more than ordinarily assumed. *Interpretation Theory*, 45.

[9]Paul Ricoeur, *Rule of Metaphor*, 47. Ricoeur observes, "This is why metaphor is more powerful [than simile]: the direct attribution causes surprise, whereas simile dissipates this surprise." While it may be a "lower form" of metaphor, simile is truly metaphorical even if it is weakened in its capacity to surprise the reader or hearer.

[10]Ricoeur, *Interpretation Theory*, 64–68.

[11]Ricoeur, *Interpretation Theory*, 68.

[12]Ricoeur writes, "true metaphors are untranslatable. ... [This] does not mean that they cannot be paraphrased, but the paraphrase is infinite and does not exhaust the innovation in meaning." *Semeia 4*, 80.

[13]Ricoeur, *Hermeneutics and the Human Sciences*, ed. and trans. John B. Thompson (Cambridge: Cambridge University Press, 1981), 18.

[14]Ricoeur, *Semeia 4*, 80. See Jacques Derrida's reservations about the distinction between "proper" and metaphorical language as well as between living and dead metaphor. "White Mythology: Metaphor in the Text of Philosophy," trans. F. C. T. Moore, *New Literary History* 6 (1975): 5–74. Claudia V. Camp summarizes Derrida's argument to stress the social and not philosophical origins of metaphors. "Metaphor in Feminist Biblical Interpretation," 15–17.

[15]Fiumara proposes that there is a tendency for us to want to manage language in a way that eliminates ambiguity. Consequently, metaphor "frequently inhabits the margins of discourse and its potential incivility generates concern for its management … an effort of *containment* and a problem of *mastery*" (*Metaphorical Process*, 3).

[16]Ricoeur, *Rule of Metaphor*, 244 and *Semeia 4*, 94.

[17]George Lakoff and Mark Johnson, *Metaphors We Live By* (Chicago/London: The University of Chicago Press, 1980), 5. Lakoff and Johnson's work has been properly criticized. See especially Mickel Bal, "Metaphors He Lives By," *Semeia 61*, 185–207 and Claudia V. Camp, "Metaphor in Feminist Biblical Interpretation," 17–20. I wish only to endorse Lakoff and Johnson's view that basic metaphors shape our daily language.

[18]Lakoff and Johnson, 232–33.

[19]Ibid., 233.

[20]Ricoeur, "The Metaphorical Process as Cognition, Imagination, and Feeling," 151–52.

[21]This is Kraftchick's summary of the work of Mary Gerhart and Allan Russell, "A Necessary Detour," 16. In this connection he speaks of how the metaphorical relationship enables one to "map" one reality by means of another (pp. 13–14). This reconceptualizing occurs as a result of the "dissonance of thought" implicit in metaphor (p. 15).

[22]Ricoeur, *Hermeneutics and the Human Sciences*, 167, 170, and 174.

[23]Ricoeur speaks of "worn-out metaphor." For example, *Rule of Metaphor*, 285. Still, elsewhere in the same work he writes, "In brief, critical consciousness of the distinction between use and abuse lead not to disuse but to re-use of metaphors, in the endless search for other metaphors, namely, a metaphor that would be the best one possible" (p. 253).

[24]Ricoeur speaks of "the *openness* of the metaphorical process" in connection with the "extravagance" of the narrative parables. That openness protects the metaphorical narrative from closure. *Semeia 4*, 99.

[25]See Ricoeur, "The Metaphorical Process as Cognition, Imagination, and Feeling," 147. With regard to both metaphor and image, I differ from Ricoeur in my use of the word "ambiguity." He maintains that "properly speaking, we are confronted with ambiguity only when one meaning alone of two possible meanings is required and the context does not provide us grounds for deciding between them." With metaphor, he continues, we encounter discourse "where several things are meant at the same time, without the reader being required to choose between them,"*Rule of Metaphor*, 91. I employ the word ambiguity (and ambiguous) more broadly to describe that multiple meaning of metaphors and images of which Ricoeur speaks. Ambiguity refers in this study to all the possible meanings of a statement, regardless of their number. See William Empson, *Seven Types of Ambiguity* (New York: New Directions, 1966), especially his description of the fourth and sixth types of ambiguity (e.g., pp. 133 and 176).

[26]Of course, the application of "family systems" to congregations has addressed this very fact. See especially the formative contribution of Edwin H. Friedman, *Generation to Generation: Family Process in Church and Synagogue* (New York: Guilford Press, 1985). See the more recent work of Ronald W. Richardson, *Creating a Healthier Church: Family System Theory, Leadership, and Congregational Life,* Creative Pastoral Care and Counseling Series (Minneapolis: Fortress Press, 1996).

[27]Suzette Haden Elgin, "Response from the Perspective of a Linguist," *Semeia 61*, 211.

[28]See, for example, Ricoeur, *Rule of Metaphor*, 247, and *Semeia 4*, 95–96.

[29]Ricoeur and others have argued that the dissimilarity of a metaphor is as important as the similarity and that the verb "to be" (i.e., the copula "is") holds that tension, e.g., *Rule of Metaphor*, 248. In his article "The Metaphorical Process as Cognition, Imagination, and Feeling," he claims that metaphor produces new meaning in the imagination "not above the differences, as in the concept, but in spite of and through the differences" (p. 146).

[30]Ricoeur, *Interpretative Theory*, 68.

[31]Kraftchick, "A Necessary Detour," 21. Here he is summarizing the discussion in Joel Winsheimer's *Philosophical Hermeneutics and Literary Criticism* (New Haven: Yale University Press, 1991). Kraftchick argues that the tension in metaphor creates something like a paradox, the "is" and "is not" being both an affirmation and negation.

[32]See Howard Clark Kee, *Who Are the People of God? Early Christian Models of Community* (New Haven, Conn.: Yale University Press, 1995). Kee argues that contemporary trends in Christian thought require recognition of their origins in the early church.

[33]See Sandra M. Schneiders, *The Revelatory Text: Interpreting the New Testament as Sacred Scripture* (San Francisco: HarperCollins, 1991). Schneiders writes, "The process of appropriation of experience is a process of 'languaging' it and, by means of language, integrating it with the rest of our experience." Scripture and tradition are appropriated through language, and languaging them is a means of participating in their meaning (pp. 70–71).

Chapter 3: "On the Way"

[1]Margaret Pamment argues that the metaphor of the way (or journey) is eclipsed in the Gospel of John by the one of "residence" (or what we call "home" in chap. 4). She writes, "What seems to have happened is that the dominant metaphor of residence has strangled 'the way' and left it motionless." "Path and Residence Metaphors in the Fourth Gospel," *Theology* 88 (1985), 118–24, quotation, p. 124.

[2]For a very good survey of the biblical use of journey in both the Old and New Testaments see Frank R. VanDevelder, *The Biblical Journey of Faith: The Road of the Sojourner* (Philadelphia: Fortress Press, 1988). VanDevelder's goal is similar to the goal of this chapter. He seeks to show the prominence of the biblical image of journey in the belief that such an image is useful to a church in a changing world.

[3]See Sandra M. Schneiders' concise summary of what she calls "Ideal Meaning Versus Authorial Intention" in *The Revelatory Text: Interpreting the New Testament as Sacred Scripture* (San Francisco: HarperCollins, 1991), 144–48. For other examples, see the work of "The Bible and Culture Collective," ed. Elizabeth A. Castelli, Stephen D. Moore, Gary A. Phillips, and Regina M. Schwartz, *The Postmodern Bible* (New Haven and London: Yale University Press, 1995), especially 1–19, and Fernando F. Segovia, ed. *"What Is John?" Readers and Readings of the Fourth Gospel*, Society of Biblical Literature Symposium Series, ed. Gail R. O'Day, no. 3 (Atlanta: Scholars Press, 1996), ix.

[4]Scripture itself employs this sort of interpretation in the sense that one biblical author interprets an earlier writing in terms of a new and contemporary situation. The easiest example might be Matthew's "fulfillment quotations" (e.g., 1:22–23). The first evangelist takes for granted that the text of Hebrew scripture is rich with new meaning as it is read and reread in new situations. See M. Eugene Boring's "Excursus: Matthew As Interpreter of Scripture" in "The Gospel of Matthew: Introduction, Commentary, and Reflections," *The New Interpreter's Bible*, Leander E. Keck, general ed., vol. 8, "New Testament Articles, Matthew, Mark" (Nashville: Abingdon, 1995), 151–54. For a more general discussion, see Robert Kysar, "Preaching as Biblical Theology: A Proposal for a Homiletic Method," *The Promise and Practice of Biblical Theology*, John Reumann, ed. (Minneapolis: Fortress Press, 1991), 143–56.

[5]To cite only two recent works that use this theme, see Bernhard Christensen, *The Inward Pilgrimage: An Introduction to Christian Spiritual Classics* (Minneapolis: Augsburg, 1996) and *Journeying Into God: Seven Early Monastic Lives*, trans. Tim Vivian (Minneapolis: Fortress Press, 1996).

[6]Harriet Crabtree, *The Quest for True Models of the Christian Life: An Evaluative Study of the Use of Traditional Metaphor in Contemporary Popular Theologies of the Christian Life*, Harvard Dissertations in Religion, 29 (Minneapolis: Fortress Press, 1991), 152–58, quotations, pp. 155 and 158, respectively.

[7]Crabtree, *The Christian Life*, 159. She cites Carol Ochs, *Women and Spirituality* (Totowa, N.J.: Rowan and Allanheld, 1983), 117, as her source for the expression "a destinationless 'walk'."

[8]Crabtree, *The Christian Life*, 160–61, quotation, 160. Martin Forward names two of the same dangers inherent in thinking of Christian life as pilgrimage: It is too personal and has too often been used in detachment from other images. "Pilgrimage: Luke/Acts and the World Religions," *King's Theological Review* 8, no. 1 (Spring 1985), 11.

[9]Crabtree, *The Christian Life*, 162.

[10]Crabtree, *The Christian Life*, 164–65, 175–89, quotations pp. 186 and 190.

[11]For example, Luke Timothy Johnson observes simply that Luke-Acts should be read as a *"single* story." *The Gospel of Luke*, Sacra Pagina, ed. Daniel J. Harrington (Collegeville, Minn.: Liturgical Press, 1991), 4. Robert Tannehill has written a fascinating two-volume work on Luke-Acts that stresses the importance of each for the interpretation of the other. *The Narrative Unity of Luke Acts: A Literary Interpretation*, vol. 1, *The Gospel According to Luke*

(Philadelphia: Fortress Press, 1989) and vol. 2, *The Acts of the Apostles* (Minneapolis: Fortress Press, 1990).

[12]As examples of the recent discussions of the literary genre of Acts, see especially the work of Richard I. Pervo, *Profit with Delight: The Literary Genre of the Acts of the Apostles* (Minneapolis: Fortress, 1987) and *Luke's Story of Paul* (Minneapolis: Fortress Press, 1989). See also Mikeal C. Parsons and Richard I. Pervo, *Rethinking the Unity of Luke and Acts* (Minneapolis: Fortress Press, 1993). They warn against easy resolutions of the problems in the relationship of the two.

[13]Scholars do not agree on the basic structure of travel narrative (9:51—19:21). Joseph A. Fitzmyer offers a simple proposal. He divides Luke 9:51—19:27 into two major parts: 9:51—18:14, in which there are no narratives that parallel Mark's, and 18:15—19:27, which seems to follow Mark's story in 10:13–52. Within the first major part Fitzmyer identifies three subunits on the basis of mentions of Jerusalem as the destination of the journey, namely, 9:51 ("set his face toward Jerusalem"); 13:22 (which literally reads "journeying toward [the] city"); and 17:11 ("on his way to Jerusalem"). *The Gospel According to Luke I-IX: A New Translation with Introduction and Commentary*, The Anchor Bible, William Foxwell Albright and David Noel Freedman, general eds., vol. 28 (Garden City, N.Y.: Doubleday and Company, 1981), 138–40. Compare R. Alan Culpepper, "The Gospel of Luke: Introduction, Commentary, and Reflections," *The New Interpreter's Bible*, Leander E. Keck, general ed., vol. 9, "Luke, John" (Nashville: Abingdon, 1995), 35–36.

[14]For example, David P. Moessner, *Lord of the Banquet: The Literary and Theological Significance of the Lukan Travel Narrative* (Minneapolis: Fortress Press, 1989; reissued Valley Forge, Penn.: Trinity Press International, 1998). Moessner contends that Luke's main purpose in both the travel section of the gospel and the whole of Acts is to show that God's promise to Israel is fulfilled in Christ and the Christian movement (see, e.g., p. 325). For a brief summary of various views of the narrative see Culpepper, "The Gospel of Luke," 11–12 and 214.

[15]Robert L. Brawley writes, "Suspense pulls readers forward in narrative like the proverbial carrot before the horse." When the eventual outcome is announced (as it is in Jesus' predications of his passion), "the narrative's enticement shifts from what will happen to how it will happen." *Centering on God: Method and Message in Luke-Acts*, Literary Currents in Biblical Interpretation, Danna Nolan Fewell and David M. Gunn, eds. (Louisville: Westminster John Knox, 1990), 34. See also Floyd V. Filson, "The Journey Motif in Luke-Acts," *Apostolic History and the Gospel: Biblical and Historical Essays Presented to F. F. Bruce on His 60th Birthday*, W. Ward Gasque and Ralph P. Martin, eds. (Exeter: Paternoster Press, 1970), 71.

[16]On the scholarly debate concerning the purpose of Luke's use of geographical references see the summary in Fitzmyer, *The Gospel According to Luke I–IX*, 164–171. I do not deny the geographical dimension of the gospel's story; it adds an earthly quality to the narrative. But I contend it does more and functions metaphorically for the reader.

[17]On the theme of reversal in Luke-Acts see the concise statement in Luke Timothy Johnson, "Luke-Acts, the Book of," *Anchor Bible Dictionary*, David Noel Freedman, ed. vol. 4 (New York: Doubleday, 1992), 417–18.

[18]The Greek verb (*epitimao*) translated "rebuke" in 9:55 is the same word the author has just used in 9:42 where Jesus "rebukes" the "unclean spirit" in a boy. Jesus commands the unclean spirit of retribution out of the disciples.

[19]For a simple discussion of this first century Jewish view and its ramifications for the church today see Robert Kysar, *Called to Care: Biblical Images for Social Ministry* (Minneapolis: Fortress Press, 1991), especially 26–28 and 44–51.

[20]On three occasions the third evangelist uses the strong verb *splagchnizomai* (translated "was filled with compassion") to identify the divine compassion for the needy: once to speak of Jesus' compassion for the grieving widow of Nain (7:13), once to describe the Samaritan's compassion for the man alongside the road to Jericho (10:33), and once to convey the quality of the father's welcome of his prodigal son (15:20).

[21]See Culpepper's succinct description of table fellowship in the Gospel of Luke. "The Gospel of Luke," 26–27.

[22]For the teachings of Luke-Acts regarding the poor see especially these volumes: Walter Pilgrim, *Good News to the Poor: Wealth and Poverty in Luke-Acts* (Minneapolis: Augsburg Press, 1981); Halvor Moxnes, *The Economy of the Kingdom: Social Conflict and*

Economic Relations in Luke's Gospel, Overtures to Biblical Theology (Philadelphia: Fortress Press, 1988); and R. J. Cassidy, *Jesus, Politics and Society* (Maryknoll, N.Y.: Orbis Books, 1978) and *Society and Politics in the Acts of the Apostles* (Maryknoll, N.J.: Orbis Books, 1987). The article on "Poor, Poverty" in *The Anchor Bible Dictionary* written by J. David Pleins and Thomas D. Hanks is also helpful, vol. 5, pp. 402–424. See especially p. 417 for a brief summary of Luke-Acts on the subject.

[23]This saying is widely supported in the gospel tradition. It has a Markan form (e.g., Mark 8:35), one that seems to have been part of the Q sayings source (e.g., Matt. 16:25// Luke 17:33), and a Johannine form (John 12:25). See Robert Kysar, *John*, Augsburg Commentary on the New Testament (Minneapolis: Augsburg Publishing House, 1986), 195–96, and *The Scandal of Lent* (Minneapolis: Augsburg Publishing House, 1982), 66–75.

[24]Forward claims the story challenges us "not to contain that vision (of God's presence) but to go from it to new insights on the way" ("Pilgrimage," 11).

[25]Moessner, *Lord of the Banquet*, 296–97. He finds summaries at the end of each of these six division. In each case they offer an assessment of the journeys just described (5:42; 9:31; 12:24–25; 15:35; 19:20; and 28:30–31), p. 297.

[26]See, for example, Filson, "The Journey Motif in Luke-Acts," 70, and Moessner, *Lord of the Banquet*, 306.

[27]The author of Acts rehabilitates the word "sign" (*semeion*) by using it in a positive way. Throughout the first three gospels the word often denotes a deed of wonder that authenticates Jesus' claims and makes faith unnecessary. Hence, the word has a negative connotation (e.g., Mark 8:11–12//Matt. 16:1–4; //Matt. 12:38–42//Luke 11:16, 29–32). Acts shares a more favorable use of the term with the Gospel of John (e.g., John 2:11; 4:54; 20:30, but see also 4:48).

[28]Moessner proposes that, like Jesus, the earliest Christians shared four "Features of the Prophet's Vocation." Both were called and sent in mission, proclaimed the "Word of the Lord," did mighty works that demonstrated prophetic authority, and received extraordinary perceptions. *Lord of the Banquet*, 51–55. Johnson claims the Christians' ability "to imitate the suffering of the Messiah" evidences the Spirit's power. *The Acts of the Apostles*, 15.

[29]See the definitive work by Luke Timothy Johnson, *The Literary Function of Possessions in Luke-Acts* (Missoula: Scholars Press, 1977).

[30]Such an idea of the replication of Jesus' ministry in that of the earliest church is further suggested by Stephen's death in Acts 7. The parallels between Stephen's death and Jesus' are obvious (e.g., Stephen's dying prayers in Acts 7:59–60 compared with Jesus' in Luke 23:34 and 46). Tannehill suggests the parallels show Stephen's faithfulness in following Jesus and how his martyrdom witnesses to Jesus' own death. *Narrative Unity: Volume 2*, 99. Johnson adds that Stephen's death demonstrates the prophetic power provided in the Spirit. *Acts*, 143. I suggest Luke-Acts teases us with the possibility that, in the sacrifices of Christians for the sake of witness, the church even continues Jesus' own suffering and death on behalf of the world.

[31]Scholars have drawn attention to the fact that Luke studiously omits the accounts in Mark of Jesus' journeys beyond Galilee or narrates those stories in unnamed or different locales (Mark 6:45 and 7:24, 31). See Fitzmyer, *The Gospel According to St. Luke I–IX*, 166. Matthew reports that Jesus orders the disciples not to go to Gentiles or Samaritans but only "to the lost sheep of Israel" (Matt. 10:5–6). The Gospel of John, however, reports a ministry of Jesus in Samaria (John 4:1–42). For uncertain and different reasons the four gospels vary in their understandings of the geographical reaches of Jesus' work.

[32]On this story see Beverly Roberts Gaventa, "Ethiopian Eunuch," *The Anchor Bible Dictionary*, vol. 2, 667. Thomas Rosica compares the gospel story of the two disciples on the road to Emmaus with that of Philip and the Ethiopian on the road to Gaza. He concludes that they are each "symbolic structures of journeys or *Ways*." The first moves through Christ to the scriptures and the second through the scriptures to Christ. "The Road to Emmaus and the Road to Gaza: Luke 24:13–35 and Acts 8:26–40," *Worship* 68, no. 1 (1994), 117–31.

[33]For this very reason, among many others, Elisabeth Schüssler Fiorenza's provocative claim that scripture provides us with a prototype and not an archetype is helpful. See, for instance, *In Memory of Her: A Feminist Theological Reconstruction of Christian Origins* (New York: Crossroads, 1983), 26–36, and *Bread Without Stone: The Challenge of Feminist*

Biblical Interpretation (Boston: Beacon Press, 1984), xvi–xvii and 9–11. Witness, too, how a prototypical approach to a text is applied by Rebecca Chopp in chapter 2 of *The Power to Speak: Feminism, Language, God* (New York: Crossroads, 1991), 40–70. Chopp prefers to speak of prototypes (in the plural) in order to indicate "the multiplicity of discourses within the Bible" (p. 143, note 8).

[34]Forward, "Pilgrimage," 9. See also David Rhoads, *The Challenge of Diversity: The Witness of Paul and the Gospels* (Minneapolis: Fortress Press, 1996).

[35]Filson argues that Acts ends in Rome in order to show that Jerusalem is dispensable for the church and to establish Rome as the church's new center. "The Journey Motif in Luke-Acts," 74–75.

[36]Gerard Genette calls the ending of Acts an ellipsis that simply characterizes the narrative of a two-year period, i.e., preaching and teaching. *Narrative Discourse: As Essay in Method* (Ithaca, N.Y.: Cornell University Press, 1980), 87–109. Cited in Brawley, *Centering on God*, 154.

[37]This is the title of the second chapter of Brawley's book, *Centering on God*, 34–57.

[38]On the much discussed "we" passages in Acts see Vernon K. Robbins, "By Land and by Sea: The We Passages and Ancient Sea Voyages," *Perspectives on Luke-Acts*, ed. C. H. Talbert, Perspectives in Religious Studies, Special Studies Series, no. 5, Watson E. Mills, ed. (Danville, Va.: Association of Baptist Professors of Religion, 1978), 215–42. Tannehill suggests the anonymous and plural first person helps us to participate imaginatively in the narratives, "to see ourselves as companions of Paul," and to heighten "our experience of the journey …" *Narrative Unity* 2: 247.

[39]The original goodness of creation is implicit in what has often been observed to be Luke's emphasis on the historical setting in Jesus' and the church's stories. That emphasis is clear, for example, in Luke 1:1–5 and 2:1–3 and in Acts 18:12–17; 23:1–8, 23–30; 23:1–8; and 25:13. The whole narrative is placed in a real sociopolitical setting that resists any effort to diminish the implicit value of history as the stage for God's saving activity. Human salvation is not achieved in some transcendent and mythical realm but in the world God created.

Chapter 4: "Homing"

[1] Paul Ricoeur, *The Rule of Metaphor: Multi-disciplinary Studies of the Creation of Meaning*, trans. Robert Czerny et al. (Toronto, Buffalo, London: University of Toronto Press, 1977), 289.

[2]John H. Elliott, *A Home for the Homeless: A Sociological Exegesis of 1 Peter, Its Situation and Strategy* (Philadelphia: Fortress Press, 1981), 230. See also pp. 236–37.

[3]Ricoeur speaks of the close relationship of symbol and root metaphor, saying the former is the "gathering together" of the meaning that makes metaphor possible. *Figuring the Sacred: Religion, Narrative, and Imagination*, ed. Mark I. Wallace, trans. David Pellauer (Minneapolis: Fortress Press, 1995), 143, also 53. Philip Wheelwright discusses the relationship of metaphor, symbol, and archetypal symbol in *Metaphor and Reality* (Bloomington, Ind.: Indiana University Press, 1962), chaps. 5 and 6. I am hesitant to speak of archetypal metaphors for two reasons. The first is that what has been claimed to be archetypical of humans is too often exclusively Western and masculine. The second reason for avoiding the use of archetype is that culture determines language as a whole.

[4]Elliott, *A Home for the Homeless*, 221. For the general importance of metaphor in biblical interpretation see Peter W. Macky, *The Centrality of Metaphors to Biblical Thought: A Method for Interpreting the Bible* (Lewiston, N.Y.: E. Mellen Press, 1990).

[5]See, for instance, Victor Paul Furnish's article on Ephesians in *The Anchor Bible Dictionary*, David Noel Freedman, general ed. (New York: Doubleday, 1992), 2: 538.

[6]Victor Paul Furnish, *II Corinthians: Translated with Introduction, Notes, and Commentary*, The Anchor Bible, William Foxwell Albright and David Noel Freedman, eds. (Garden City, N.Y.: Doubleday, 1984), 32A, 295. Furnish warns against imposing a body-soul distinction on Paul or reading him as if he speaks here of life after death. The perspective is that of two ages. The present one is temporary and the one to come eternal (pp. 293–95).

[7]Again Paul's perspective is of two ages. See C. K. Barrett, *The First Epistle to the Corinthians*, Henry Chadwick, ed., Harper New Testament Commentary, 2d edition (New

York: Harper and Sons, 1971), 370–78. For a fuller discussion see Hans Conzelmann, *1 Corinthians: A Commentary on the First Epistle to the Corinthians*, trans. James W. Leitch, Hermeneia—A Critical and Historical Commentary on the Bible, George W. MacRae, S.J., ed. (Philadelphia: Fortress Press, 1975), 280–93. Conzelmann points out that Paul cannot conceive existence without a body (p. 280).

[8]See C. Freeman Sleeper, *The Victorious Christ: A Study of Revelation* (Louisville: Westminster John Knox, 1996).

[9]See, for example, Elisabeth Schüssler Fiorenza, *The Book of Revelation: Justice and Judgment* (Philadelphia: Fortress Press, 1985), especially 50–51 and 68–76, as well as *Revelation*, Proclamation Commentaries, Gerhard A. Krodel, ed. (Philadelphia: Fortress Press, 1991), especially 129–131.

[10]Elliott, *Home for the Homeless*, 23, quotation, pp. 48–49.

[11]Elliott, *Home for the Homeless*, 220–37, quotation, p. 233. Troy W. Martin faults Elliott for reading 1 Peter's metaphors literally. Martin identifies "Diaspora" as the controlling metaphor of the epistle. Around that central metaphor are three clusters of other images: "Elect household of God," "aliens in this world," and "the sufferers of the dispersion." *Metaphor and Composition in 1 Peter*, Society of Biblical Literature Dissertation Series, David L. Petersen and Pheme Perkins, eds., no. 131 (Atlanta: Scholars Press, 1992), 142–266.

[12]See, for example, Jerome H. Neyrey, *An Ideology of Revolt: John's Christology in Social-Science Perspective* (Philadelphia: Fortress Press, 1988). Neyrey suggests that Christians interpreted their view of Christ in terms of their actual social situation. On the role of social and cultural methods of interpreting scripture in relation to other interpretative methods, see Vernon K. Robbins, *Exploring the Texture of Texts: A Guide to Socio-Rhetorical Interpretation* (Valley Forge, Pa.: Trinity Press International, 1996).

[13]Two other uses of "family of faith" (Gal. 6:10) or "household of God" (1 Tim. 3:15) demonstrate the way in which the early Christians were encouraged to fashion their communities of faith in terms of households. Interestingly, in both of these passages the authors are urging proper Christian behavior. However, the so-called household codes (Col. 3:18—4:1; Eph. 5:21—6:9; 1 Peter 2:11—3:12; 1 Tim. 2:8–15; 5:1–2; 6:1–2; and Titus 2:1–10; 3:1) admonish Christians to adhere to certain social duties as practiced in their culture. (See the article, "Household Codes" by David L. Balch in *The Anchor Bible Dictionary* 3, 318–20.) They suggest that Christian households themselves are to conform to cultural values. As such, these passages hint at how some Christians communities, at least, found cultural practices consistent with life in Christ. Elliott contends that the household duties in 1 Peter 2:11–3:12 suggest that "identity" and "integration" are "key terms for describing the social needs of the Christian sectarians." *Home for the Homeless*, 208–20, quotation, p. 219.

[14]Elliott, of course, agrees that 1 Peter fostered a sectarian mentality among its recipients. See, e.g., *Home for the Homeless*, 75.

[15]Stanley Hauerwas and William H. Willimon exploit the image of the church as "resident aliens" in *Resident Aliens: Life in the Christian Colony* (Nashville: Abingdon Press, 1989) and *Where Resident Aliens Live: Exercises for Christian Practice* (Nashville: Abingdon Press, 1996). My reservation about their work entails a nagging suspicion that their portrayal comes perilously close to being sectarian. Nonetheless, they develop the image with important consequences.

[16]Ernst Käsemann, *The Wandering People of God: An Investigation of the Letter to the Hebrews*, trans. Roy A. Harrisville and Irving L. Sandberg, 2nd German ed., 1957 (Minneapolis: Augsburg Publishing House, 1984), 17–48, quotations, pp. 19 and 44, respectively. The book was first published in 1938 while Käsemann was a pastor to miners and first drafted when he was imprisoned by the Nazis for his resistance to their rule. He admits in a preface to the second German edition that the book is dated and that much research on Hebrews has succeeded it (pp. 15–16).

[17]On the relationship between metaphor and model see Max Black, *Metaphors and Models* (Ithaca, N.Y.: Cornell University Press, 1962) and Ricoeur's interesting use of Black's analysis in *Rule of Metaphor*, 87–88 and 243–44 as well as *Semeia 4: Paul Ricoeur on Biblical Hermeneutics*, John Dominic Crossan, ed. (Missoula: Scholars Press, 1975), 85.

[18]Robert Kysar, *John*, Augsburg Commentary on the New Testament, Roy A. Harrisville, Jack Dean Kingsbury, and Gerhard A. Krodel, eds. (Minneapolis: Augsburg Publishing House, 1986), 266.

[19]See Raymond E. Brown, S.S., *The Gospel According to John (I–XII): Introduction, Translation, and Notes*, The Anchor Bible (Garden City, N.Y.: Doubleday and Company, 1966), 510–12.

[20]See, for instance, my expression of Ernst Käsemann's proposal (*The Testament of Jesus According to John 17*, trans. Gerhard A. Krodel [Philadelphia: Fortress Press, 1968]) in *John, the Maverick Gospel*, rev. ed. (Louisville: Westminster John Knox, 1993), 102. See also R. H. Gundry, "'In My Father's House are Many *Monai*' (John 14:2)," *Zeitschrift für neutestamentliche Wissenschaft*, 11 (1967), 68–72.

[21]Gail O'Day, "The Gospel of John: Introduction, Commentary, and Reflections," *The New Interpreter's Bible*, Leander E. Keck, general ed., vol. 9 (Nashville: Abingdon, 1995), 740–41. Of 14:2 I wrote, "While this promise has to do with the heavenly existence of the believers, there is also a sense that this relationship is realized in the association of Christ with his church." Kysar, *John*, 221.

[22]This interpretation is found in Kysar, *John, the Maverick Gospel*, 115 and is once again dependent on Käsemann's provocative reading of John 17 in *Testament of Jesus*.

[23]For a fuller analysis of this view see Kysar, *John, the Maverick Gospel*, 99–106.

[24]D. Moody Smith puts it this way: "In John the character of the future expectation has changed because of the past, historic advent of Jesus Christ and the presence of the Spirit in the community, but the view of the nature of the world and its continuing bondage in darkness has not." *The Theology of the Gospel of John*, New Testament Theology, James D. G. Dunn, general ed. (Cambridge: Cambridge University Press, 1995), 85.

[25]See J. Massyngbaerde Ford's provocative thesis in *Redeemer–Friend and Mother: Salvation in Antiquity and in the Gospel of John* (Minneapolis: Fortress Press, 1997).

[26]See, for example, Gail O'Day, "Johannine Theologians as Sectarians" and Robert Kysar, "Coming Hermeneutical Earthquake in Johannine Interpretation," *What Is John? Readers and Readings of the Fourth Gospel*, Society of Biblical Literature Symposium Series, Gail R. O'Day, ed. no. 3 (Atlanta: Scholars Press, 1996), 199–203 and 185–89, respectively. For an important study of the social world of the Gospel of John see David Rensberger, *Johannine Faith and Liberating Community* (Philadelphia: Westminster Press, 1988).

[27]For this view of biblical authority, I am indebted both to an unpublished paper by Elizabeth Huwiler entitled "Ministry in Daily Life: Perspectives from the Old Testament and Reconstructions of Ancient Israel/Judah," and my conversation with her as a result of her paper. Huwiler's initial proposal entailed allowing the Israelite and Judahite traditions to dialogue as equal partners rather than repressing the former as the Old Testament itself often attempts to do.

Chapter 5: "Stumbling in the Light"

[1]I am indebted for this phrase to the stimulation of the title of an article by Jeffrey L. Staley, "Stumbling in the Dark, Reaching for the Light: Reading Character in John 5 and 9." Staley argues that neither of the characters in these two chapters is portrayed without weaknesses, and I believe such a portrayal is an apt description of the life of the church. *Semeia 53: The Fourth Gospel from a Literary Perspective*, R. Alan Culpepper and Fernando F. Segovia, eds. (Atlanta: Scholars Press, 1991), 55–80.

[2]For example, Elie Wiesel, *Night*, trans. Stella Rodway (New York: Bantam Books, 1960), speaks of a horror that haunts any of us who have struggled with evil.

[3]The expression was a first title Anselm used for what he later entitled Proslogium (i.e., a discourse). *St. Anselm: Basic Writings*, trans. S. N. Deane, 2d ed. (LaSalle, Ill.: Open Court Publishing Co., 1962), 1.

[4]See Robert Kysar, *1-2-3 John*, Augsburg Commentary on the New Testament, Roy A. Harrisville, Jack Dean Kingsbury, and Gerhard A. Krodel, ed. (Minneapolis: Augsburg Publishing House, 1989), 35–40, 81, and 115–16.

[5]See Dwight M. Smith, *The Theology of the Gospel of John*, New Testament Theology, James D. G. Dunn, general ed. (Cambridge: Cambridge University Press, 1995), 85.

[6]Consult the essays in *Images of Jesus Today*, James H. Charlesworth and Walter P. Weaver, eds. Faith and Scholarship Colloquies 3 (Valley Forge, Penn.: Trinity Press International, 1994). My concern in this section, and in the whole of this study, is not to distinguish within the gospels between the historical Jesus and the church's Christ of faith.

Such an effort is fraught with methodological problems. I will speak of Jesus as the character represented to us in the gospel texts without concern for the historical accuracy of those representations. See Luke Timothy Johnson, *The Real Jesus: The Misguided Quest for the Historical Jesus and the Truth of the Traditional Gospels* (San Francisco: HarperSanFrancisco, 1996).

[7]However, among others, David E. Garland thinks Matthew's use of "heaven" instead of "God" is more profound than a simple act of piety. "The kingdom of heaven is favored (over kingdom of God) because it is a way of referring to God's transcendent work and lordship that is coming down from heaven ..." *Reading Matthew: A Literary and Theological Commentary on the First Gospel*, Reading the New Testament Series (New York: Crossroad Publishing Co., 1993), 47.

[8]On the background of the kingdom of God, see G. R. Beasley-Murray, *Jesus and the Kingdom of God* (Grand Rapids, Mich.: Wm. B. Eerdman's Publishing Co., 1986), 3–68, and Petr Pokorny, *The Genesis of Christology: Foundations for a Theology of the New Testament*, Marcus Lefébure, trans. (Edinburgh: T & T Clark, 1987), 15–22. Marc Zvi Brettler's study *God Is King: Understanding an Israelite Metaphor*, Journal for the Study of the Old Testament, Supplement Series 76 (Sheffield: Sheffield Academic Press, 1989) is a helpful study of the royal metaphor Israel used for God.

[9]Norman Perrin, *Jesus and the Language of the Kingdom: Symbol and Narrative in New Testament Interpretation* (Philadelphia: Fortress Press, 1976), 15–33, quotation pp. 32–33. Perrin employs Philip Wheelwright's distinction between "steno" and "tensive" symbol. The former has a one-to-one equation with that which it represents (e.g., as with mathematical symbols), while the latter functions much like a poetic metaphor in that it stimulates endless possibilities of meaning. Philip Wheelwright, *Metaphor and Reality* (Bloomington, Ind.: Indiana University Press, 1962). See also Paul Ricoeur, *The Symbolism of Evil*, trans. Emerson Buchanan, Religious Perspectives, ed. Ruth Nanda Anshen, vol. 17 (New York: Harper and Row, 1967). On the relationship of symbol and metaphor see Ricoeur, *Figuring the Sacred: Religion, Narrative, and Imagination*, Mark I. Wallace, ed., David Pellauer, trans. (Minneapolis: Fortress Press, 1995), especially 53 and 143.

[10]For example, John Dominic Crossan contends, "The kingdom movement was Jesus' program of empowerment for a peasantry becoming steadily more hardpressed ..." This was so, Crossan argues, because the phrase *kingdom of God* "evokes an ideal vision of political and religious power, of how this world here below would be run if God, not Caesar, sat on the imperial throne." *The Essential Jesus: Original Sayings and Earliest Images* (San Francisco: HarperCollins, 1994), 7–8 and 12.

[11]For a discussion of this passage and its meaning see R. Alan Culpepper, "The Gospel of Luke: Introduction, Commentary, and Reflections," *The New Interpreter's Bible*, Leander E. Keck, general ed., vol. 9 (Nashville: Abingdon Press, 1995), 329–30.

[12]G. B Caird, *Theology of the New Testament*, completed and edited by L. D. Hurst (New York: Oxford University Press, 1994), 129, quotation, p. 118. See also Werner Georg Kummel, *The Theology of the New Testament According to Its Major Witnesses: Jesus, Paul, John*, trans. John E. Steely, trans. (Nashville: Abingdon Press, 1974), 33–37.

[13]For insights into this passage see these works: Mary Ann Tolbert, *Sowing the Gospel: Mark's World in Literary-Historical Perspective* (Minneapolis: Fortress Press, 1989), 160–61; Donald H. Juel, *Mark*, Augsburg Commentary on the New Testament (Minneapolis: Augsburg Publishing House, 1990), 70–72; John Paul Heil, *The Gospel of Mark as Model for Action: A Reader-Response Commentary* (New York and Mahwah, N.J.: Paulist Press, 1992), 99; and Paul J. Achtemeier, *Mark*, Proclamation Commentaries, Gerhard Krodel, ed. (Philadelphia: Fortress Press, 1975), 57–59.

[14]See the seminal work of Jack Dean Kingsbury, *The Christology of Mark's Gospel* (Philadelphia: Fortress Press, 1983). The secret of the kingdom is, I believe, clearly linked to the secret of Jesus' identity in Mark. But it is also associated with the apocalyptic reversal that occurs in the crucifixion—that is, in the mystery of God's plan for the final triumph over the forces of evil. See Joel Marcus, *The Mystery of the Kingdom of God*, Society of Biblical Literature Dissertation Series, ed. J. J. M. Roberts and Charles Talbert, no. 90 (Atlanta: Scholars Press, 1986), 229–32.

[15]On the basis of Luke 12:32 David L. Tiede claims, "Thus, the 'seeking' for the kingdom ... (v. 31) is interpreted in terms of a gift...God's way of ruling in heaven and on earth has been revealed to proceed from God's gift and grace." *Luke*, Augsburg Commentary on

the New Testament (Minneapolis: Augsburg Publishing House, 1988), 237–38. See also Frederick W. Danker, *Jesus and the New Age: A Commentary on St. Luke's Gospel*, rev. ed. (Philadelphia: Fortress Press, 1988), 251–52.

¹⁶Bernard Brandon Scott, *Hear Then the Parable: A Commentary on the Parables of Jesus* (Minneapolis: Fortress Press, 1989), 8.

¹⁷On the metaphorical quality of Jesus' parables see Paul Ricoeur, *Semeia 4: Paul Ricoeur on Biblical Hermeneutics*, John Dominic Crossan, ed. (Missoula: Scholars Press, 1975), 37–145. Ricoeur defines a parable as "the mode of discourse which applies to a *narrative form* a metaphorical process"(p. 88). See also J. Dominic Crossan, "Parable," *The Anchor Bible Dictionary*, David Noel Freedman, ed., vol. 5 (New York: Doubleday, 1992), 146–52. Crossan defines a parable as "An extended metaphor or simile frequently becoming a brief narrative, generally used in biblical times for didactic purposes" (p. 146). Norman Perrin calls a parable "an extended metaphor," which bears within itself the reality to which it refers. *Jesus and the Language of the Kingdom*, 56. See also his discussion on pp. 132–68 and 194–204. Against the view that parables are a kind of metaphor, see Charles W. Hedrick, *Parables as Poetic-Fictions: The Creative Voice of Jesus* (Peabody, Mass.: Hendrickson Publishers, 1994), especially 29–33. Hedrick also rejects the notion that Jesus' parables originally referred to the kingdom of God (pp. 4, 9, and 28). In nearly every way, however, Hedrick's reading of the parables as poetic fictions parallels what I understand to be the role of metaphor.

¹⁸Scott writes, "In narratives where there is strong dissimilarity to the expected values of the referent, as there frequently is in Jesus' parables, dissimilarity may well be a way of redefining and subverting a hearer's vision of the referent so as to redescribe reality." *Hear Then the Parable*, 51.

¹⁹Hedrick, *Parables as Poetic Fictions*, 32–35.

²⁰Scott points out that titling a parable "unconsciously and unknowingly provides the reader with a definite perspective on the parable." For that reason he retitles all the parables he treats by using the first line of the story. *Hear Then the Parable*, 4. Titles seem to me to close or at least narrow the parables' meanings, but I nonetheless use the traditional titles as an expedient way of informing the reader of the passage to which I am referring.

²¹John R. Donahue, S.J., writes of this parable: "Hardly any parable in the Gospels seems to upset the basic structure of an orderly society as does this one." The grumbling workers "are so enclosed in their understanding of justice that it becomes a norm by which they become judges of others. They want to order the world by their norms which limit the master's freedom and exclude unexpected generosity." *The Gospel in the Parables: Metaphor, Narrative, and Theology in the Synoptic Gospels* (Minneapolis: Fortress Press, 1988), 81–82. David E. Garland's comments on the parable are similar: "It confounds those who expect justice from God…This parable therefore offends anyone who believes that hard work pays off and who looks at salvation as a payoff." *Reading Matthew*, 204–5. See also Bernard Brandon Scott, *Hear Then the Parable*, 297–98. Dan Otto Via, Jr., has a slightly different interpretation of the discontented workers: "Because of their impenetrable legalistic understanding of existence, grounded in the effort to effect their own security, they exclude themselves from the source of grace." *The Parables: Their Literary and Existential Dimension* (Philadelphia: Fortress Press, 1967), 154.

²²David E. Garland says, "Matthew is a Gospel that emphasizes the doing of righteousness; but this parable shows that Matthew also understands the scandalous nature of God's grace." *Reading Matthew*, 206.

²³For Joseph A. Fitzmyer this is the key for unlocking the parable's puzzle. *The Gospel According to Luke X—XXIV: A New Translation with Introduction and Commentary*, The Anchor Bible, William Foxwell Albright and David Noel Freedman, eds., vol. 28A (Garden City, N.Y.: Doubleday and Co., 1985), 1095–96. See also J. D. M. Derrett, "Fresh Light on St. Luke xvi:I. The Parable of the Unjust Steward," *New Testament Studies*, 7 (1960–61), 198–219 (reprinted in Derrett, *Law in the New Testament* [London: Darton, Longman and Todd, 1970], 48–77).

²⁴Some see this parable as an example story of action in the midst of crisis. For example, Eduard Schweizer, *Good News According to Luke*, trans. David E. Green (Atlanta: John Knox Press, 1984), 254–55 and Frederick Danker, *Jesus and the New Age*, 279–80. Others pair it with the previous parables in chapter 15 and suggest it has to do with freedom from fearful servitude to God (e.g., Donahue, *The Gospel in the Parables*, 165–69). Still others understand it to be sarcasm (e.g., Tiede, *Luke*, 281–83). At least one interpreter wonders if it

really is a bit of comic relief and fosters a willingness to laugh at our own seriousness (Via, *The Parables*, 162).

[25]Bernard Brandon Scott, *Hear Then the Parable*, 255–66, quotation pp. 265–66.

[26]Actually, "kingdom of God" is but one instance of Jesus' use of metaphor and figurative speech. All four of the gospels portray Jesus as a poetic teacher-preacher. Bernard Brandon Scott explores this characteristic in *Jesus, Symbol-Maker for the Kingdom* (Philadelphia: Fortress Press, 1981) in which he concludes Jesus' "language is consistently tensive" and compels faith (pp. 167–77). Robert W. Funk also stresses that the "rhetorical strategies of Jesus" are frequently filled with paradoxical tension. *Honest to Jesus: Jesus for a New Millennium*, A Poleridge Press Book (New York: HarperCollins, 1996), 149–56.

[27]See, for instance, Sandra M. Schneiders, *The Revelatory Text: Interpreting the New Testament as Sacred Scripture* (San Francisco: HarperCollins, 1991), 27–33. For another discussion of the role of metaphor in theology in general and in Paul in particular, see Robert G. Hughes and Robert Kysar, *Preaching Doctrine for the Twenty-First Century*, Fortress Resources for Preaching (Minneapolis: Fortress Press, 1997), 20–35 and 59–73.

[28]See Gordon D. Kaufman's important work *The Theological Imagination: Constructing the Concept of God* (Philadelphia: Westminster Press, 1981). In contrast to the imaginative nature of theological language, some decades ago many tried to understand religious language in relationship to ordinary descriptive language. For example, see Ian T. Ramsey, *Religious Language: An Empirical Placing of Theological Phrases*, The Library of Philosophy and Theology (London: SCM Press, 1957) and Frederick Ferré, *Language, Logic and God* (New York: Harper and Row, 1961).

[29]For many of us the awakening began with Mary Daly, *Beyond God the Father: Toward a Philosophy of Women's Liberation* (Boston: Beacon Press, 1973). For a sampling of the literature critical of God language from a feminist perspective see Sallie McFague, *Metaphorical Theology: Models of God in Religious Language* (Philadelphia: Fortress Press, 1982), 215. A brief and accessible treatment is found in Patricia Wilson-Kastner, *Imagery for Preaching*, Fortress Resources for Preaching (Minneapolis: Fortress Press, 1989).

[30]Sallie McFague, *Metaphorical Theology*, 20. See also McFague, *Speaking in Parables: A Study in Metaphor and Theology* (Philadelphia: Fortress Press, 1975) and *Models of God: Theology for an Ecological, Nuclear Age* (Philadelphia: Fortress Press, 1987).

[31]Rebecca S. Chopp suggests that the loss goes even further. She argues that it is not enough simply to acknowledge metaphors and create new ones. She maintains that "symbolic ordering" underlies our metaphors and that the reformation of that order is more important than merely changing our metaphors. *The Power to Speak: Feminism, Language, God* (New York: Crossroad, 1991), 111–12. Claudia V. Camp makes a related point in "Metaphor in Feminist Biblical Interpretation: Theoretical Perspectives," *Semeia 61: Women, War, and Metaphor: Language and Society in the Study of the Hebrew Bible*, Claudia V. Camp and Carole R. Fontaine, eds. (Atlanta: Scholars Press, 1993).

[32]See Hans Dieter Betz, "Paul" (p. 187) and Ruth Majercik, "Rhetoric and Rhetorical Criticism" (p. 711) both in *The Anchor Bible Dictionary*, vol. 5.

[33]See Joseph A. Fitzmyer, *Romans: A New Translation with Introduction and Commentary*, The Anchor Bible, vol. 33 (New York: Doubleday, 1993), 614–15.

[34]Steven J. Kraftchick, "A Necessary Detour: Paul's Metaphorical Understanding of the Philippian Hymn," *Horizons in Biblical Theology: An International Dialogue* 15, no. 1 (June 1993), 1–37, quotation, p. 29.

[35]For a good and accessible discussion of Paul's use of tradition see Calvin J. Roetzel, *The Letters of Paul: Conversations in Context*, 3d ed. (Louisville: Westminster John Knox, 1991) and the older treatment found in Archibald M. Hunter, *Paul and His Predecessors* (Philadelphia: Westminster Press, 1961).

[36]See Hendrikus Boers, *The Justification of the Gentiles: Paul's Letters to the Galatians and Romans* (Peabody, Mass.: Hendrickson, 1994).

[37]Eric H. Wahlstrom, *The New Life in Christ* (Philadelphia: Muhlenberg Press, 1950), x–xvi. See also Herbert M. Gale, *The Use of Analogy in the Letters of Paul* (Philadelphia: Westminster Press, 1964). Fitzmyer calls the language Paul uses to describe Christ's benefits for humans "images." *Romans*, 116–24. On the metaphorical use of slavery terminology see S. Scott Bartchy's article in *The Anchor Bible Dictionary*, vol. 6, p. 72. One scholarly study is Dale Martin, *Slavery as Salvation* (New Haven: Yale University Press, 1990).

[38]On reconciliation in Paul and redemption as a metaphor see G. B. Caird, *New Testament Theology*, completed and edited by L. D. Hurst (Oxford: Oxford University Press, 1994), 156–58.

[39]For a brief discussion of the practice of adoption in biblical times, as well as its metaphorical use in scripture, see Frederick W. Knobloch, "Adoption," *The Anchor Bible Dictionary*, vol. 1, 76–79. For a scholarly study of adoption see James M. Scott, *Adoption as Sons of God: An Exegetical Investigation into the Background of HUIOTHESIA in the Pauline Corpus*. Wissenschaftliche Untersuchungen zum Neuen Testament, 2. Reihe, 48 (Tübingen: J. C. B. Mohr, 1992).

[40]For both a brief introduction to the debate and the Jewish background for Paul's use of "justify," see Fitzmyer, *Romans*, 116–19. Fitzmyer also summarizes the argument that Romans 3:21–26 contains a pre-Pauline formula (p. 342). John H. P. Reumann, *Righteousness in the New Testament. With Responses by Joseph A. Fitzmyer and Jerome D. Quinn* (Philadelphia/New York: Fortress/Paulist Press, 1982) exemplifies the ecumenical discussion of justification.

Chapter 6: Sowing the Seeds

[1]In my opinion the best discussions of empowerment are found in Loren Mead's proposals for transformation, especially *Transforming Congregations for the Future* (New York: The Alban Institute, 1994), chap. 3.

[2]See the classic statement of becoming in Gordon W. Allport's *Becoming: Basic Considerations for a Psychology of Personality*, Terry Lectures (New Haven: Yale University Press, 1955).

[3]I believe the best recent book on the authority of scripture, and the one most relevant to this study, is Darrell Jodock, *The Church's Bible: Its Contemporary Authority* (Minneapolis: Fortress Press, 1989). Jodock addresses the issue of scriptural authority for the church in a postmodern age. See also Kysar, *Opening the Bible* (Minneapolis: Augsburg Press, 1999).

[4]See, for instance, Donald K. McKim, *The Bible in Theology and Preaching: How Preachers Use Scripture* (Nashville: Abingdon Press, 1994). McKim catalogs the various views of biblical authority and how each of those views is expressed in preaching. My own recent effort to demonstrate some of the issues in contemporary biblical interpretation is "Living at the Epicenter: Preaching and Contemporary Biblical Interpretation," *Taproot: The Journal of the Lutheran Theological Southern Seminary* (forthcoming).

[5]For instance, the Bible presents a variety of views of suffering. Which should we take as definitive? See Daniel J. Simundson, *Faith Under Fire: Biblical Interpretations of Suffering* (Minneapolis: Augsburg Publishing House, 1980).

[6]Mike Regele and Mark Schulz ask "What Must Die?" in the future church. Among other things they list "The Obsession with Bombproof Certainty of Truth." But, interestingly, they go on in the same list to name the "radical relativism" that has too frequently reduced the gospel message to just another religious idea in our culture. *Death of the Church. The Church Has a Choice: To Die as a Result of Its Resistance to Change or to Die in Order to Live* (Grand Rapids, Mich.: Zondervan Publishing House, 1995), 204–5.

[7]Helpful suggestions for responding to this situation are found in Thomas H. Troeger, *Ten Strategies for Preaching in a Multi-Media Culture* (Nashville: Abingdon Press, 1996).

[8]It is interesting that the word translated "rebuke" (*epitimao*) is the word sometimes used of Jesus' commanding demons (e.g., Mark 1:25; 9:25). Peter and Jesus are trying to call out the demon each thinks possesses the other!

[9]In the fall of 1997 my colleague Professor M. Thomas Thangaraj preached a provocative sermon on this text in a chapel service at Candler School of Theology. He asked why it was Jesus asked the disciples, "Who do people say that I am?" (Mark 8:27) before asking them who they believed him to be. Thangaraj's point was that what others believe about Jesus is important and that we need first to consider their views before making our own confession. In a pluralistic society, such attentiveness to the views of those who differ from us is essential to the formation of faith. This kind of treatment of the confession at Caesarea Philippi provides a congregation with an incentive to deal constructively with the pluralism of our culture and to globalize its perspective. For further provocative insights

from this preacher, see Thangaraj's book, *The Crucified Guru: An Experiment in Cross-Cultural Christology* (Nashville: Abingdon Press, 1994).

[10]See the still provocative and helpful discussion of doubt and faith in Paul Tillich's classic, *The Dynamics of Faith* (New York: Harper and Brothers, 1957). Tillich writes, "doubt is a necessary element in (faith). It is a consequence of the risk of faith" (p. 18).

[11]See Robert Kysar, *John,* Augsburg Commentary on the New Testament, Roy A. Harrisville, Jack Dean Kingsbury, and Gerhard A. Krodel, eds. (Minneapolis: Augsburg Publishing, 1986), 307–8.

[12]For further reflections on preaching theological themes, including views of the church, see Robert G. Hughes and Robert Kysar, *Preaching Doctrine for the 21st Century,* Fortress Resources for Preaching (Minneapolis: Fortress Press, 1997), 113–22.

[13]The first challenge facing the church, Loren Mead believes, is the transfer of its ownership from clergy to laity. *Five Challenges for the Once and Future Church* (New York: Alban Institute, 1996), chap. 1.

[14]Harriet Mary Crabtree, *The Quest for True Models of the Christian Life: An Evaluative Study of the Use of Traditional Metaphor in Contemporary Popular Theologies of the Christian Life,* Harvard Dissertations in Religion, no. 29 (Minneapolis: Fortress Press, 1991), 186.

[15]Marilyn Kay Stulken, *Hymnal Companion to the Lutheran Book of Worship* (Philadelphia: Fortress Press, 1981), 450.

[16]Harry E. Fosdick, "God of Grace and God of Glory," *The Lutheran Book of Worship* (Minneapolis: Augsburg Publishing House and Philadelphia: Board of Publication, Lutheran Church in America, 1978), 415.

Index of Scriptural Citations